Congratulations, you're gonna be a Dad!

Congratulations, you're gonna be a Dad!

What's Ahead from A to Z for First-Time Fathers

PAUL & PAM PETTIT

Revised and Expanded

Kregel
Publications

Congratulations, You're Gonna Be a Dad! What's Ahead from A to Z for First-Time Fathers

© 2002, 2014 by Paul and Pam Pettit

Published by Kregel Publications, a division of Kregel, Inc., 2450 Oak Industrial Drive NE, Grand Rapids, MI 49505.

978-0-8254-4351-0

Printed in the United States of America
14 15 16 17 18 / 5 4 3 2 1

In loving memory of
Edward R. Pettit
(1936–1994)

Contents

A to Z 21

feature articles

Preface

Why We Wrote This Book

It's been more than ten years since the first edition of this book was released. Since that time we've spoken to countless couples who have been helped by this work. Our initial impetus for writing this birthing primer for dads was confirmed. Lots of young women told us they grew up playing with baby dolls or acting out "family" playtime situations. However, few dads ever tell us they grew up changing diapers on their baby doll or acting out "breastfeeding" with their buddies. For first-time fathers finding out you are going to be a dad can be a scary situation. Know that this book has now encouraged many men just like you. We have received letters and emails from men who tell us this work helped them move from frazzled to confident in their new role. And now our hope is that a whole new generation of expectant fathers will similarly be encouraged to become Dynamic Dads. We thank God for this second edition and trust He will use it to help build healthy families.

Many men who are about to become fathers feel they're on their own. Their fathers may have been physically or emotionally absent, causing what family experts call a "father wound." We all have this father wound to some extent. If you've suffered abuse, neglect, or absence, then your father wound may be a deep and painful one. Or perhaps you've been blessed with an involved, loving dad. No matter what your dad was like, your own fathering efforts will be affected by his example. If that example was healthy, your own children will be blessed. But if it left something to be desired, you'll need to make a concerted effort to avoid repeating your father's mistakes. Either way, read on. Our message is one of hope! You can stop a cycle of poor fathering or continue to build on a legacy of healthy fathering—it's your decision.

Being a good dad begins by taking an early and active role in your baby's life. This involvement begins with how you treat your wife during pregnancy and will intensify the closer you get to d-day (delivery day). This is no time for fear! This is a job for a real man. A real man helps his wife when her ankles are swollen and her back hurts. A dynamic dad helps his wife through the pain of labor and delivery. Moreover, an engaged father holds his newborn close—very close—and whispers in his little baby's ear, "I'm your daddy, and I love you. You're safe in my arms; I'm going to take care of you."

Being masculine includes changing diapers and warming bottles in the middle of the night. The truly masculine man enters into his newborn's world and explores it with his baby, seeing the world through his baby's eyes.

Expectant dads sometimes think, "I can't get down on my hands and knees and coo and crawl with my baby! I'll feel like a sissy!" That's the kind of thinking that deepens the father wound. Unfortunately, when dads think this way the cycle is perpetuated, and the pain of longing for an involved father continues.

A baby who never receives the touch and attention of a loving dad will go through life wondering, "What's wrong with me?" If you think we're exaggerating, consider this striking statistic: In the first eighteen months of life, gender identity is formed. That's right! Before the first two years have sped by, an infant is able to distinguish the subtle differences between his father's and mother's voices, heartbeats, smell, and even their skin! Before babies can even say "Dada" or "Mama," they've already locked into their brain the thought *this is Mom* or *this is Dad*. You are genuinely needed from day one. So prepare now to physically and emotionally enter into your newborn's world.

Reading this book is a further step in becoming a dynamic dad. Now, from day one, every chance you get, plan to hold your baby, pray for your baby, read to your baby, talk to your baby, change your baby, and enter into his or her world. Reject passivity! Fight through the father wounds you may have experienced, and lovingly move *toward* your baby—toward your very own generous gift from God. Emotionally healthy men make better fathers. Trust us on that.

Introduction

Why You Should Read This Book

Welcome to the greatest roller coaster ride of your life. Whether you've just discovered you're expecting or are several weeks into the pregnancy, strap yourself in for a bumpy ride of changing emotions and attitudes. At times you'll experience the heights of euphoria and excitement. At other times, different thoughts (*What if something goes wrong? How much is all this going to cost?*) could plunge you into sheer terror. But here's a little secret: This range of emotions is quite normal. In fact, it's expected.

Many men feel threatened by merely thinking of a new baby. While most men feel secure in performing what they know—jobs, household responsibilities, hobbies—how many are adept at quieting a fussy baby or bathing a newborn? Many books address the care of toddlers, and numerous books offer advice to the expectant mother. But this book is for you—the father. It focuses on the delivery and care of your newborn and is written from a father's perspective.

An entire generation of fathers stood alone in a waiting room or hallway while their sons and daughters were born. And we're certain many of you have not sat with your father or an older man to ask all the various questions on your mind: Will my wife begin to totally ignore me? What will happen to our sex life? Am I capable of attending to the needs of an infant? Will I be able to provide financially for my growing family?

This book addresses such questions with frank, direct answers. And it offers encouragement to you, the new dad. It is arranged alphabetically by topic and is interspersed with articles authored by well-known—and not-so-well-known—fathers. You'll be encouraged as you read these stories. Think of them as advice from experienced dads to one just learning the ropes—you.

Refer to this book as questions arise during pregnancy, delivery, and as your baby grows. Some information is of a medical nature, some is humorous, and some will prompt you to take specific steps to prepare for d-day (delivery day). Part of the advice is just plain common sense, confirming your gut feelings. Always consult your obstetrician-gynecologist (ob-gyn)—or pediatrician, once the baby arrives—if you have serious medical questions. There is no such thing as a dumb question. Although a plethora of medical advice is available in books and on the Internet, we still strongly encourage you to ask your specific questions of your own physician.

Why has God blessed you with a baby? Because He knows you can handle the job. The gift of fatherhood helps you become more and more the man He wants you to become. Being a father means you are growing in patience, servanthood, boldness, character, and a host of other virtues. At times you'll look heavenward and wonder, "Why did You give me this baby?" Whether that question arises out of pleasure or pain, the answer will be the same: "Because I love you, and I want you to experience all that being a father entails."

We trust this book will encourage you as you learn how millions of men before you have survived the expectant-dad roller coaster ride. So step in line and strap yourself in. Congratulations, you're gonna be a dad!

Pregnancy Timeline

0–4 weeks

Pregnancy lasts approximately forty weeks. It's best to wait until the end of the first trimester (third month of pregnancy) to announce the impending birth. At that stage, the chance of a miscarriage decreases. Until then, enjoy the secret the two of you share. Now that your doctor has confirmed your good news, your wife should avoid hot baths, alcohol, cigarette smoke, caffeine, and heavy lifting. While she should also avoid taking over-the-counter medications, your doctor will most likely prescribe prenatal vitamins. Your wife may also begin to feel morning sickness around this time. You should be extra sensitive to her nausea and offer help and comfort.

5–8 weeks

Now's the time to start planning your calendar. You and your wife should discuss work-related concerns—time off, vacations, maternity leave, and insurance. This is also a great time to shop for baby items and room decorations, before it becomes uncomfortable for your wife.

During a doctor's appointment in the coming weeks, you may be provided an opportunity to hear your baby's heartbeat. The end of the third month is the official end of the first trimester, at which point many women report their morning sickness diminishes. Others remain nauseous off and on throughout. During the coming months, support your wife with walks, visits to the doctor, back massages, and general encouragement.

Word of your impending arrival will soon begin to spread. Talking with experienced parents and grandparents can lessen fear of the unknown.

9–12 weeks

If you are planning to take a pre-birth class, now is the time to enroll. Many local hospitals and community agencies offer helpful, fun classes that meet for a few weeks. At this time, your doctor may perform certain tests to check on the health of your baby. Your wife may begin to show, and her body will change shape. Her breasts will probably become larger, and her tummy may be expanding. Now is not the time for wisecracks regarding her figure! By the end of the third month, your baby is approximately two inches long and weighs about an ounce.

12–14 weeks

At this time, consider names and housing situations. Do you need to replace your sports car with a minivan? Be prepared for a variety of emotions during this stage. If your wife is feeling up and happy one day and down and fearful the next, she has a perfectly fine case of the normals.

Now is not the time to clam up. Be sure to talk with her during this time. You and your wife should be experiencing this pregnancy *together.* Many men begin to work harder during the pregnancy, feeling that they need to provide financially for their new family. But your long hours at the office or worksite can frustrate your wife, who may feel she is going through the ordeal alone. Stand by her side.

14–16 weeks

Tests, tests, and more tests. This is the time when some important screens are performed to check on the health of your baby. Two of the most common are the maternal serumalpha-fetoprotein (MSAFP) screening and the multiple marker test. Your doctor is checking for problems such as spina-bifida and high sugar levels. Be patient. The results of these tests normally take a few days, and waiting can be difficult. Assure your wife that no matter the results, you are going through the pregnancy and birth as a committed team. Your baby is still small enough at this stage to fit into the palm of your hand, yet he or she is sensitive to light and sounds and even gets the hiccups!

17–20 weeks

You're almost halfway to d-day! Mom may be feeling the baby move. Your wife's body is really changing now. Because her stomach is being pressed upward, she may experience heartburn as well as an aching back almost daily. If you wonder why, imagine what it would be like to reduce the size of your stomach by half, strap ten to twenty pounds onto your gut, and then walk around like that *all day*. If you haven't already done so, take on more of the household chores. Bending and lifting are proving to be uncomfortable if not difficult for your wife. It's common, too, for moms to experience constipation and swollen ankles at this stage.

Also, if you haven't done so, tell your supervisor and coworkers about your future work schedule. Nowadays it is normal for a new dad to take time off for delivery, recovery, and settling the baby into the home. While almost all moms will take maternity leave, more and more new dads are taking paternity leave. Yes, it's *that* important.

21–24 weeks

Does your wife mention how tired she is all the time? She's not joking. The baby is literally pulling iron, minerals, and blood from her body. And her expanding uterus is pushing up against her lungs, so she may be out of breath after even a short walk. Since Baby is relying heavily on Mom's diet, you can help her out by eating healthy as well. Practice skipping the fast foot and eat more vegetables, fruits, and protein-rich foods. Your baby is now approximately eight inches long and weighs about a pound. Dad, are you praying for your wife, the delivery, and the arrival of your new son or daughter?

25–28 weeks

Someone may give a shower party for the baby. Put off buying too much baby equipment, because others may give you these items as gifts. Week twenty-seven is the last week your wife should travel by air without approval from your doctor. Your wife will now want to eat several small meals throughout the day as opposed to three full meals. And she will want to stand and stretch throughout the day and evening. For more comfortable sleeping, she may want to surround herself with several large, soft pillows. You may begin to practice breathing and relaxation exercises at this point. You can also now discover the sex of your baby.

29–32 weeks

Start planning some of the details for your trip to the hospital. Have you received or purchased an infant car seat yet? You can't leave the hospital without one. Have you considered having someone in the delivery room with you? Whom do you want? What do you want the environment to be? Celebrative? Reflective? Many of the choices are up to you. As a supportive husband, you may at this time increase the back rubs, trips to purchase frozen yogurt, and extra efforts at household chores. Are your cell phone and/or video camera ready to roll if you desire to use them?

33–36 weeks

Your baby can now arrive at any moment. Your wife will begin to experience Braxton-Hicks, or involuntary muscle contractions in the tummy, pelvic, and back region. It's time now to purchase infant diapers, baby shampoo, lotions, and basic baby supplies. Your wife may want to purchase a nursing bra. Have you planned for someone to help in the home in the days following the delivery? Do you want someone to stay at your home? If so, whom? Have you done some advanced food and household shopping? Do you know the best route to the hospital? At this stage, your doctor or hospital may allow you to log into a web-based text or message system that allows you to provide instant access to the delivery room. Focus now on how your life is about to change; for a new dad, there's no turning back now.

37–40 weeks

Most doctors will not allow your baby to progress past the forty-week mark. If you are in the fortieth week, you are probably hours away from delivery. Your wife's amniotic fluid (water) may or may not "break." In the last stages of the fortieth week, your doctor may advise your wife to walk around to "get things going." If things do not progress, your doctor may use medications to stimulate labor. Once you arrive at the hospital, everything happens very quickly. We advise new dads to try to be "fully present." Get into the situation at hand and soak it all in. What time is it? How does your wife look and feel? Has the baby "dropped" into the birth canal? Is it too bright or too loud in the room? Are you feeling weak or strong? Once the heavy labor begins and your baby's head "crowns," there are only a few precious moments until you are fully a new dad. Congratulations! Welcome to fatherhood! Here is a social media security alert: Don't announce, "We're heading to the hospital for a few days. We're so excited!" Unfortunately, this could be an invitation for some unscrupulous characters to break into your home. It's sad but true.

following delivery

At first, your baby may look unusual to you. He or she will probably be wet, wrinkled, and covered with vernix (a wax-like substance) and might not look anything like what you had imagined. Don't put off moving toward your baby. Begin to bond this instant, not a year or two from now. Hold your baby, talk to him or her, and look into your baby's eyes.

Activity around the home will be hectic for a few days, but don't let that keep you from your baby. Spend time holding and walking with Baby. Don't let the busyness of having visits from friends and relatives keep you from enjoying these first days as a new family. These are moments and days you will never get back. And in the first few days, your baby will change so much. Seemingly overnight, his or her eyes will come into focus, and hand and arm movements will become more coordinated. Everyone will be exhausted, but it will be a good kind of exhaustion. The days and years that stretch out in front of you can be left for someone else to worry about right now. Celebrate the new life God has placed into your life. Smile . . . dance . . . go outside and jump up and down. Go to a restaurant and announce you want "the new dad special." Call an old friend whom you haven't seen in a while and shout into the phone, "My wife and I just had a baby!" Praise the Lord.

Behold, children are a gift of the LORD.
—Psalm 127:3 NASB

air travel (*see also* vacations)

Some airlines prohibit travel for Mom after the seventh month of pregnancy. Airlines do a great job of delivering passengers and packages, but they don't specialize in delivering babies. Always consult your doctor regarding any travel—including car, bus, or train trips—in the days and weeks leading up to your due date. After your baby is born, you may desire to take him or her to visit family or friends. When traveling by air, plan ahead to relieve potential pain in your baby's eardrums caused by the pressure changes in the cabin. Always bring something for Baby to suck on—a bottle or pacifier helps relieve the pressure. Long flights are difficult. Some passengers may become annoyed if your baby is fussy. By the end of the flight, you may be the one with the pacifier in your mouth.

announcements (*see also* welcome, yard sign)

Many couples send or post birth announcements for family and friends, sharing the good news. Items to include are date and time of birth; Baby's birth weight and length; Mother's condition; description of Baby; and any other notes you deem newsworthy, such as a brief account of the events leading up to and surrounding the delivery. Be creative. You could send a picture or include a favorite verse of Scripture. When you state your baby's full name, it's fun for readers to know why you chose a particular one, so the definition of an unusual name or the family connection of a middle name can be included.

anomaly

This word is used by the medical community when referring to a problem or abnormality during pregnancy. Some problems are minor and require little attention. Others are treatable with medicine or bed rest. The worst tragedy possible would be losing your baby or wife during the pregnancy or delivery. Some anomalies can be diagnosed early during a routine sonogram or ultrasound. A problem can, however, go undetected until the actual delivery. You must be as mentally and physically prepared as possible to deal with any complications that arise.

Someone may ask how a good and loving God could allow a tragedy to occur. The fact is, no one knows why God allows us to experience heartbreaking circumstances. Trust that God will give you comfort and strength. He never gives us more than we can handle. Remember, He has promised us, "Be strong and courageous. Do not be afraid or terrified . . . for the LORD your God goes with you; he will never leave you nor forsake you" (Deut. 31:6). Isn't that a great promise!

Apgar score

Dr. Virginia Apgar created an assessment tool for newborns. Using her last name as an acronym, she developed a scale for the following categories:

    A–Appearance (color)
    P–Pulse (heartbeat)
    G–Grimace (reflex irritability)
    A–Activity (muscle tone)
    R–Respiration (breathing)

Since you may be wondering how your newborn is really doing, ask a nurse or doctor, "What was the Apgar score?" The baby will be scored at one minute and five minutes after birth. A score of seven or above will let you know your baby is doing great. A score of four or below means your baby may need special attention from the medical staff. In addition, you'll make yourself appear really knowledgeable. The nurses in the hallway will say, "The dad in room 117 asked for his son's Apgar score! He really knows his stuff!"

areola

Your wife's body is going through enormous hormonal and physical changes. Her breasts are becoming larger, and the ring surrounding the nipple, the areola, is becoming darker. Veins will appear due to the increase in circulation required for breastfeeding. Most women report that their breasts are tender, even painful to the touch. When breastfeeding is done properly, your baby will take much of the areola into his or her mouth.

attitude

Be honest with yourself. What is your attitude toward your baby? Do you talk to the baby in the womb? Are you afraid your wife will give all of her attention to the baby to the point of ignoring you and your needs? Are you fearful of what may happen in the delivery room? During your prayer time, be brutally honest with God regarding any inadequacies you are feeling. Talk with your wife about these concerns.

You may want to seek the advice of your pastor, father, or another man who has wrestled with some of these same concerns. Seek out a man who has witnessed a couple of deliveries and ask him to recount his experiences. Spend some time in conversation with an older man who has successfully raised a few children.

Know that the attitude you bring into the delivery room will have a big impact on your wife. Your role is coach, comforter, and encourager. You will need to be strong for her if she becomes physically weak or emotionally fragile.

The quote below from Chuck Swindoll is known as simply "the attitude quote." You may have seen it on T-shirts, posters, restaurant menus, coffee mugs, or key chains. Read it slowly and deliberately, and consider: What is your attitude toward your upcoming role as father?

Words can never adequately convey the incredible impact of our attitude toward life. The longer I live the more convinced I become that life is 10 percent what happens to us and 90 percent how we respond to it.

I believe the single most significant decision I can make on a day-to-day basis is my choice of attitude. It is more important than my past, my education, my bankroll, my successes or failures, fame or pain, what other people think of me or say about me, my circumstances, or my position. Attitude keeps me going or cripples my progress. . . . It alone fuels my fire or assaults my hope. When my attitude is right, there's no barrier too high, no valley too deep, no dream too extreme, no challenge too great for me.

(Taken from *Strengthening Your Grip* by Charles R. Swindoll, copyright 1982, Charles R. Swindoll. Used by permission of W Publishing Group, Inc., Nashville, Tennessee.)

....

Bassinets, Beached Whales, and Braxton-Hicks
Charlie Dyer

Thoughts on the birth of a child were etched in black and white . . . and came straight from the original *Dick Van Dyke Show*: Laura, stylish with a small pillow around the waist to simulate pregnancy, calls calmly to her husband; Rob leaps from bed, fully dressed in his rumpled suit, shouting,

"Oh my goodness, it's time!" Mysteriously, Laura somehow just "knew" when it was time to head to the hospital, and Rob only had to keep from coming apart at the seams as he waited in nervous anticipation.

Then the time approached for my wife to give birth to our son . . . and I learned what television neglects to tell us!

Bassinets

For most men, shopping is a necessary evil. We know that a baby will require some new equipment, but usually we don't have a clue as to what it is. And we don't want to waste our weekends wandering through aisles of bassinets, cribs, and strollers.

I soon learned, however, about the "nesting instinct." It kicks in at some point during pregnancy, and it will become vitally important for your wife to have a place prepared for her first child. And you need to be involved, because it assures her that you care for her and that you are concerned about her needs. So smile, don't complain, and prepare yourself for the fascinating world of baby furniture.

Beached Whales

One major difference between pregnancy on the *Dick Van Dyke Show* and pregnancy in real life is the self-perception of the mother-to-be. On the show, Laura looked stylishly plump in her designer clothes, perfectly coifed hair, and matching shoes. In reality, most women in their final months of pregnancy feel more like Moby Dick than Laura Petrie. They are so uncomfortable that they are willing to go through just about anything to unload the sack of potatoes around their waist that keeps kicking them in the ribs.

Your wife may not feel attractive or desirable during her final trimester, so make sure you are especially sensitive during this time. Here's a list of dos and don'ts for the average male.

Do	Don't
Offer to rub her legs, back, or neck when she gets a cramp or is in pain.	Make any references to Moby Dick or the Goodyear blimp.
Help her turn over in bed and scratch in places she can no longer reach.	Complain if she no longer has the energy to do everything she could do before.
Tell her you love her and think she is beautiful.	Compare her to others and say, "Well at least you're not as fat as _____!"
Let her place your hand on her stomach to feel the baby kick.	Be grumpy if she decides to deliver at 3 AM.

The list could go on, but I think you get my point. Your wife may not feel too special or physically attractive as the time for the birth approaches. Let her know through your words and your deeds that you think she's special.

Braxton-Hicks

On the television show, Laura says to her husband, "Rob, it's time," and off they go to the hospital to have their baby. Real life bears no resemblance to television. The watchword during our final few weeks of pregnancy was Braxton-Hicks, often called false labor.

Your fear is, of course, that somehow your wife will go into labor and you won't make it to the hospital on time. Your recurring nightmare has you delivering the baby on the side of the highway . . . with rush hour traffic crawling by . . . and the traffic helicopter hovering overhead broadcasting pictures of the event. (Okay, so this might not be your recurring nightmare, but I'll bet you're still concerned about getting to the hospital on time.)

When contractions first begin, your wife has no way of knowing whether or not she is experiencing Braxton-Hicks contractions or the "real thing." This can be stressful for her and for you, but your reaction can add to her stress or help to alleviate it. Don't panic. Don't get upset. Don't expect her to be able to tell you whether it's false labor. The best thing you can do is be calm and reassuring, and start timing the frequency and duration of the contractions. If there's any question, call your doctor.

If it turns out to be Braxton-Hicks, don't get upset with your wife for waking you up in the middle of the night . . . or having you miss part of the game of the week on television . . . or making you leave work just before an important meeting with your boss. She can't tell whether it will be false labor or the real thing, and you don't want her to be unwilling to share with you what is happening. Recognize that this is going to happen, and roll with the punches.

The approaching birth of your child is a time of insecurity, uncertainty, and unexpected interruptions. Your wife will be looking to you for comfort, help, and encouragement. Make a commitment now to be the support she needs. You will never regret it!

Dr. Charlie Dyer is professor-at-large of Bible at Moody Bible Institute in Chicago, Illinois, and serves as the host of the radio program The Land and the Book.

B

babysitters

No doubt you and your wife will soon want to venture out without your newborn. Who will watch your baby? If no close friends or family members are immediately available, you may need to hire a babysitter. Screen all applicants. Do they know how to administer CPR? Could they assist in a choking incident? Here is a checklist to leave for the sitter: cell phone number, phone number for the place you will be, phone numbers of neighbors, specific instructions for care of your baby, and time you expect to be home.

It's a good idea, too, to post a list—perhaps on the refrigerator—that includes your baby's name, date of birth, home address, family doctor's name and number, and other vital information, just in case the need arises to call 911.

balloons (*see also* flowers)

The decor in some hospital rooms is downright drab. Although you may stay only a short time, balloons help to brighten up the place. They also look great as backdrops for the pictures and video you will take. Balloons may be purchased at most hospital gift shops, florists, or grocery stores (latex balloons, because of severe allergies, may be banned from some hospitals). The sight of a new dad wheeling his wife and baby out of a hospital with balloons tied to the wheelchair is a beautiful picture of life, hope, and promise. Older babies and toddlers love balloons, so you'll often see them at birthday parties or other celebrations. Always be sure to dispose of balloons properly so a baby does not chew or choke on one.

bathing

It takes a brave man to bathe a newborn. Many new dads are fearful of dropping or drowning their infant. Caution is recommended here. When babies are wet, they are slippery and hard to hold. If you've ever thrown a football in the rain, you know what we mean. It helps to use a towel or washcloth to hold Baby.

The first few days after birth, a portion of the umbilical cord will still be attached. Try to keep this area dry. In fact, don't give Baby a tub bath until the umbilical cord is off and the belly button is healed. Babies do not need tub baths every day. Always make sure the water is not too hot. Your baby's skin is much more sensitive than yours and can easily be burned or scalded. Never put a newborn's head under water.

To bathe, gently wash around the eyes and eyelids first, while the washcloth is still clean. Next, clean in and around the ears. Do not use cotton swabs in the ears. Wash the rest of the body with baby soap and water, being careful to wash skin creases and folds well. Wash the hair last with baby shampoo (shampoo that contains a very low pH balance) and dry it well with a towel. Do not use a blow dryer to dry the baby's hair as a blow dryer can get too hot and can burn your baby's sensitive scalp. Finally, dry the baby and wrap him or her in a warm blanket.

After bathing, you can apply a baby lotion if needed. While your baby is very young, use an unscented lotion and don't put lotion on the baby's head. It is best not to use baby powder or talc, as it can be harmful if the baby breathes it in. And remember—never, ever leave a baby of any age unattended around water.

bilirubin

Bilirubin is a by-product of the normal breakdown of old red blood cells. Too much bilirubin causes a fairly harmless type of jaundice in about 50 percent of newborns, because their young livers can't metabolize it quickly enough. When this by-product stays in the bloodstream, it can cause the baby's eyes and skin to become yellow. The medical term for jaundice is *hyperbilirubinemia*. Ultraviolet rays can help break down bilirubin, so your doctor may prescribe treatment with lamps or direct sunlight. If you are concerned that your baby's skin is too yellow, always consult your doctor. Harmful levels of bilirubin create a condition called *kernicterus* (the staining of certain areas of the brain by bilirubin). This could lead to cerebral palsy and hearing loss.

birth control (*see also* ob-gyn, tubal ligation, vasectomy)

As you near delivery, your ob-gyn will probably talk with you about family planning. Some couples opt for no contraception of any form. Others desire to "space" future children two or three years apart. Know that it is possible to conceive just days after returning home from the hospital after giving birth. Don't think you can't get pregnant because "we just had a baby" or "my wife is breastfeeding." Obviously, contraception is a highly personal matter you and your wife will need to discuss and agree upon. Remember that God is the giver of life. Although we might plan and prepare for children, God grants conception in His own timing.

Your doctor will more than likely recommend abstaining from sexual intercourse for six weeks while Mom's body heals. Talk with your doctor about the use of oral contraceptives while breastfeeding. Remember, issues surrounding birth control can be highly controversial. Many hold highly charged opinions on this sensitive subject.

birthing room (*see also* maternity room)

Most birthing centers and hospitals are equipped with the technical equipment and trained staff you need for a successful delivery. We do not recommend delivering your baby at home. The possibility of complications always exists, and specialized training is required to handle intricate problems. Seconds can mean the difference between life and death for your wife or child. Many hospitals are making a transition from the stark antiseptic birthing rooms of the 1950s and 1960s toward the more relaxed, comfortable LDR (labor/delivery/recovery) rooms. These rooms include rocking chairs, couches, televisions, stereo systems, and muted color schemes. Some hospitals even allow siblings or other family members to be present during delivery. A couple of months before your due date, you should make an appointment with your hospital to tour a birthing room.

Items you may want to bring to the birthing room include lotion to rub on your wife's back, a favorite musical selection of songs, your wife's overnight suitcase packed with her personal items, and an object such as a picture or hourglass to focus upon. Some women report that focusing upon a lava lamp helps them to lose track of time and concentrate on proper breathing. Some moms enjoy hearing their husband read special passages from the Bible. Dad, you may want to pack a few snacks or juices so you can remain in the room with Mom. Another good idea is to pack a list of phone numbers of special friends and family members to call after the delivery. Men, it's not a good idea to get involved in a sporting event or show on TV. As the labor pains increase, the last thing your wife wants to hear is, "But honey, they're in the ninth inning!" or "Yeah, sweetie, I hear you. I know it hurts, but it's the fourth quarter. I'll be there in a second." Not a good idea at all.

blood (*see also* queasiness)

Prepare yourself emotionally and physically to see blood during the delivery. Many men report a feeling of helplessness during the final series of contractions. As a loving husband, you may want to take all of your wife's pain away. Some men become faint and actually pass out. During delivery, a nurse may ask you, "Dad, you still with us?" If you know you get squeamish around blood or when seeing your wife in pain, let the nurses know ahead of time and they will assist you. This is in no way an admission of weakness. It would be far worse if, while passing out, you fell and hit your head or injured yourself in some way, leaving you out of commission. Your wife and new baby will need you after the delivery, so try to make it through safely. You may be standing on your feet for what could be hours at a time, so take breaks and eat properly. One hint: pack a lunch or a snack in an overnight bag. Again, you won't want to miss the delivery because you were waiting in line at the hospital cafeteria or "slipped out" to pick up pizza.

blues (*see also* postpartum depression)

It's normal for you or your wife to go through a time of mild depression, often called the "baby blues," in the days following the homecoming of your baby. During delivery, adrenaline was coursing through your veins as you rode the roller coaster of emotions that surround this most intense of times. Now your vision may become cloudy. All you see are dirty diapers and hospital bills. The helpers you had at home right after your baby was born may no longer be with you. In other words, you're feeling overwhelmed.

These are common feelings and are even to be expected. You and your wife need to give each other breaks. Go for a long run or walk. Have a date night out. Take a day off from work and do something fun. This mild depression should fade in a week or two. If it does not, tell your doctor; it could be postpartum depression, a more serious condition that requires medical attention. The worst thing you can do is keep these feelings bottled up. Parenthood is difficult at times. There may be days when you feel as though you can't take the next step. Open up to a friend or neighbor, and don't be shy about asking for help.

bonding

We can't stress enough the importance of early father attachment, or bonding, with your newborn. Bonding is, in essence, the basis of this entire book. The results of one study showed that fathers who wanted to help in their child's delivery were those who had attitudes favoring parental involvement when the child was one year old. Another study showed that dads who avoided diapering and toilet training hindered their child's optimal psychosexual development. So roll up your sleeves, Dad, and get involved. Holding, cuddling, bathing, diapering, talking, and singing to your newborn all help with bonding. While holding your newborn may feel the same as holding a sack of potatoes, research shows that your baby's brain can be imprinted from the earliest moments with your specific voice patterns and even your own bodily smell.

bottle-feeding (*see also* formula, nipple confusion)

You may use bottles for feeding your baby either formula or breast milk that has been frozen and thawed. These bottles must be kept clean by thoroughly washing them in very hot water and soap to kill bacteria, then allowing them to air-dry. Most bottles can be washed in the top rack of your dishwasher. Always sterilize new bottles and nipples before their initial use. It is not necessary, as was once thought, to completely sterilize bottles after each use.

Always check the nipple to make sure the milk is flowing properly. Tip the bottle when feeding so no air is sucked in unnecessarily. Different sizes of nipples and bottles are used as Baby grows. Don't allow your baby to go to bed with a bottle, as milk could flow through the Eustachian tubes into the middle ear, causing an ear infection. When feeding a newborn with a bottle, place one of your fingers under Baby's chin for support. After weeks of feedings, you may get sick of seeing bottles. But remember—*you* like eating, don't you?

breastfeeding (*see also* frozen breast milk, nipple confusion, nipples)

Volumes have been written on this important topic. The American Academy of Pediatrics recommends breastfeeding for one year. Of course you can elect to breastfeed longer than this should you choose. Breastfeeding your infant provides him or her with significant immunity against infection. Other advantages of breastfeeding may include economy, convenience, and a more rapid recovery of Mom's uterus.

Breast-fed babies often eat every two to three hours. Some babies may nurse eight to ten minutes on each breast from the beginning. As the dad, you may feel this is not your area. It is. You will need to help with breastfeeding in many ways, especially if your wife uses a breast pump. Many women who work outside the home, or those who are involved in activities that disrupt a baby's feeding schedule, often rent or purchase breast pumps. Learn how to help. You will become adept at both storing and thawing out frozen breast milk.

In the middle of the night, you may need to get out of bed and bring Baby to your wife's side. Encourage your wife to drink lots of water and to avoid drinks with alcohol, caffeine, or large amounts of sugar. You will notice that certain foods your wife eats—such as spicy food or foods that give her gas (e.g., cauliflower or broccoli)—may upset your baby's stomach. Dad, help create a quiet spot in the home where breastfeeding can be enjoyed instead of rushed.

How do you know if your baby is getting enough milk? Follow these four rules of thumb: First, your baby seems satisfied after eating. Second, he or she wets six to eight diapers a day. Third, your baby is gaining weight. And fourth, he or she sleeps between feedings.

If you feel your baby is not eating enough or gaining the proper weight, quickly consult your doctor. Taking your baby in for this reason in no way makes you a bad dad. In fact, good parents are concerned enough about their baby's weight to have it checked often.

breathing (*see also* Lamaze classes)

Breathing delivers oxygen throughout the body. Hard labor becomes more difficult when your wife holds her breath or forgets to take deep breaths due to the pain. As in weight lifting, one needs to take deep, even breaths throughout the exercise. One of your main roles during labor will be helping your wife with her breathing during contractions. A variety of methods are employed to slow breathing to an even, steady pace. The most common is a 1, 2, 3, pause . . . 1, 2, 3, pause system, breathing in on the 1 and 2 count and breathing out on the 3 count. The breathing would sound like this: hee, hee, hoooo, pause; hee, hee, hoooo, pause. Practice this ahead of time and don't worry if you feel foolish or silly. Remember, the only thing that matters during labor and delivery is the health of your baby and wife.

breech position

When your baby's feet or legs rather than the head are facing the cervix, your baby is considered to be in a breech presentation. Sometimes a doctor can massage or reposition a baby into a "head down" presentation before delivery. If not, a cesarean section may be necessary.

burping

If you don't learn to burp your baby properly, you'll be in for some long, sustained crying and cleanup. Obviously, babies' stomachs are small. Any air trapped inside is uncomfortable for them. About halfway through a feeding, or when Baby seems disinterested in any more sucking, put Baby up on your shoulder and pat his or her back.

Firm pats on the back press the baby's tummy against your shoulder and force air out. You can also lay Baby across your lap to burp, or you may sit Baby up and support the head with your hand and pat his or her back to burp. Some babies will let out a loud burp and that will be all. Others will let out a series of small burps. Over time, you will learn when to go back to feeding. Don't forget, it's easy for *you* to burp, but your newborn needs help.

···

Introduction to Fatherhood
Howard Hendricks

You've been told that the most emotionally stressful event in a man's life is the birth of his first child. My own experience backs up that bit of wisdom.

What guy in love ponders the maternity ward? You see the most beautiful and attractive creature who ever crossed your path. You've got to have her, and you go after her pell-mell. In my case, it took five years of strategizing, straining, struggling, and stroking—to say nothing of plundering my bank account. At last I stood beside her, in front of a church full of people, after which I was assured I could legally take her home with me.

Actually our "home" was two thousand miles removed from the church. We were a "student couple" and blissfully happy. When she, who was always wholesomely healthy, told me she wasn't feeling well, I suggested some extra sleep. She'd get over it; it was just the usual adjustment to Texas.

When she didn't get over it, I concluded it was all in her head and told her so. The doctor said it wasn't in her head but in her tummy. She was headed for motherhood. Sounded okay to me. But I was an only child, so the word *pregnancy* was foreign to me. No big deal; women had been having babies since the beginning of time. It's an honorable event. Why not us? But when the baby was born, I felt left out, as if this little infant had burst in and stolen my wife. Little did I know I needed life education, and my Father in heaven was enrolling me in His "Fatherhood 101."

Back in those yesteryears when I was a rookie dad, I thought fathering meant taking turns with night feedings and paying pediatrician bills. I learned quickly it had more to do with praying with my family and learning to just be there for my wife and children—even when I'd really rather have been playing handball with my buddies. The only worthwhile legacy of a dad is what he gives away of himself to the mind and heart of a child, which, in turn, prepares that child for his or her own life.

My own dad did not know God personally until shortly before his death, yet he left his mark all over me. His words, along with body language and inflections, still play like old movies in my conscience: "Don't ever let me hear you talk to a woman like that!" "You never, never do anything dishonestly, d'ya understand?" "Son, that's not good enough when your name is Hendricks!" "Think, son, how is this job going to look when we get finished?" You see, he cared too much about me to let me get away with anything ungentlemanly or shoddy or lacking integrity.

Dad often seemed harsh and uncompromising to me, and I know I have perplexed my own children at times in the same way. But if a man is to prepare his children for the dangerous and jagged road ahead, he must teach and demonstrate how to maneuver, persistently encouraging a proper reaction to the obstacles. Love always does that which is best for the other. A good father mentors his children; he walks inside their heads and leaves his footprints on their hearts. Then, when he is gone, they will be just like him.

Dr. Hendricks (1924–2013) served as distinguished professor and chairman of the Center for Christian Leadership at Dallas Theological Seminary.

C

car seat

Attention! Your vehicle must be equipped with an infant car seat in order to take your baby home from the hospital. It's the law. Plan ahead, because you don't want to spend homecoming day driving around town looking for the best deal on a car seat. Your wife will appreciate your taking the time to shop with her. Be sure the car seat is age-appropriate and fastened securely. Check with your local Department of Motor Vehicles to find out all necessary requirements. Infant car seats should be put in the backseat and faced toward the back of the car. This is called *rear facing*. You may want to take a rolled-up blanket to help support your baby's head against the seat. Before placing your baby in the car seat, feel the metal buckles to make sure they are not hot. Never leave your baby alone in a car. Practice securing and releasing your car seat at home before your baby's homecoming so you feel comfortable operating it that day. Remember, your baby will quickly grow, so you will need to adjust the seat belts and car seat accordingly every few months.

cell phone

During the last thirty days of pregnancy, anything can happen, so you and your wife should stay in constant communication. Check in with her often to see how she's feeling. You never know when you're going to get the green light to "start your engines." Keep your cell phone by your side and charged at all times.

cesarean section (C-section)

Whether planned or not, a C-section requires special medical attention. Neonatal nurses who work with premature babies will often aid in these deliveries. When a C-section is required, the mood in the delivery room will become much more serious, and Mom will be wheeled into a surgical room. An incision will be made in the abdomen, and the physician will reach in and pull out the baby. Some couples feel cheated by a C-section, thinking they were somehow deprived of a vaginal or "normal" delivery, but these couples must realize that the health of the mother and baby is the only thing that matters. If your doctor determines that a cesarean is needed, and all the options have been explained to you, don't hesitate to get the baby out. Approximately one out of five babies is born via cesarean. The procedure is normally performed after labor has begun. If things are not moving along or if your baby is in distress, every second counts in saving the baby or Mom. If a C-section is necessary, your wife may stay an extra day or two in the hospital. Once home, she will require extra recovery time and will experience difficulty climbing stairs and getting in and out of bed.

childproofing (*see also* kitchen safety)

Before bringing Baby home, be sure to walk through your entire house to prepare for your new arrival. You have probably become comfortable with the surroundings in your house. This is about to change. Most men are shocked by the disruption a tiny baby brings to a routine. Could any of the electrical cords be tripped over in the middle of the night? Which chair will you use for bottle- or breast-feeding? Where will you bathe Baby?

As your baby grows, even more questions arise. Do you have any dangerous cleaning agents, chemicals, or medicines lying around?

Are any drapery or vertical blind cords exposed? Are your electrical outlets covered? Some safety experts recommend getting down on your hands and knees and crawling throughout your house. This will put you at a toddler's eye-level and may help you spot a potential problem. Begin now to childproof your home.

Have you thought about how your pet will react to your infant? Animals can prove dangerous to an infant through attack, allergies, or just plain curiosity.

Keep ipecac in your medicine cabinet just in case chemicals are accidentally ingested. If it ever happens, always call the poison control center first to receive instructions.

choking

Few things in life are scarier than seeing your infant choking. Would you know what to do in a choking situation? Do not stick your fingers into a choking baby's mouth. Hold the infant with his or her tummy facing the floor, head tilted downward. Give several firm open-handed pats on Baby's back. This should dislodge the object. Above all, take a childbirth preparation course that teaches CPR and how to deal with choking. Require any babysitter or caregiver to have training in CPR and choking. You will often be alone with your baby, and you need to know emergency procedures. One time, Pam showed me how to perform the procedure outlined above. The very next day, one of our children choked on a corn chip, and I knew they couldn't breathe. My first reaction was to want to put my fingers in their mouth and throat and attempt to remove the chip. However, I did exactly as Pam had said. Our baby coughed once and the chip came flying out. That was a frightening experience for me, and I was thankful I had learned the proper procedure the day before!

cigars

It's an old tradition to pass out cigars to family, friends, and coworkers after having your baby. In today's smoke-free environment, you may want to pass out fruit, chocolate, bubble gum cigars, or some other token of your joy. This memento lets everyone know of your good news and alerts them that you may be on a tentative schedule for the next few days.

circumcision

Circumcision is a minor surgical procedure in which the foreskin is removed from the head of a male baby's penis. This procedure is rooted in religious and social practice, and its medical significance has come into question. Whether to circumcise is an issue you should decide beforehand by talking with your doctor and with other parents of boys, since it is done almost routinely a day or two after delivery. If you decide to circumcise, your doctor will instruct you on caring for the circumcision site. Know that there are strong opinions on this issue, and not everyone will agree with your decision. However, it is your own decision to make as parents.

colic

If your baby cries during or following feedings on a regular basis, you may be dealing with colic. Colic has been described as pain in the intestines caused by spasms. It may be caused by reflux (bringing swallowed milk back up through the esophagus), which causes burning and irritation. One cause may be your wife eating the wrong foods. Spicy foods and breastfeeding do not mix well. If your baby continually cries surrounding feeding time, contact your pediatrician at once. There is no need to feel frustration and keep Baby in continual pain. Over-the-counter anti-gas medicine drops can help. If you find your infant is lactose intolerant, you may need to switch to a specific type of formula. Colic is emotionally draining to parents as well as Baby, so schedule breaks by finding someone who will watch your baby for a few hours at a stretch. You will be a better caregiver if you are emotionally healthy.

Some experts report that one in five babies will have some form of colic. None of our first four babies had colic. When number five rolled around, we had pretty well developed a routine as far as feeding and sleeping. Boy, were we shocked when our fifth was diagnosed with colic. He cried all the time. He was the Colic King. We now have a new appreciation for the stress caused by this malady. We listened to every remedy known to modern and ancient man. Entire websites are devoted to sharing horror stories about colic. If your baby cries for long periods for seemingly no reason, check with your pediatrician. Colic can sometimes be confirmed by a series of upper gastrointestinal tests.

colostrum

Colostrum is a thick yellowish liquid, and it is the first milk that is produced after delivery. Colostrum is very high in protein and contains antibodies that offer protection against infections. A bit of colostrum may leak out of the nipple in the final months of the pregnancy during sexual foreplay or at other times. Your wife can purchase nursing pads that will keep colostrum from staining dresses and blouses.

conception (*see also* fertility, infertility)

One of your sperm has penetrated and fertilized one of your wife's eggs, and a not-so-subtle event has occurred. God has performed a miracle in your midst. The two of you have found yourselves pregnant. Yes, the two of you. Dad, think of yourself as expecting a baby. Although you won't go through all the physical and emotional changes your wife will experience, you will go through some. Some men even report feeling morning sickness. Others feel tired all the time due to sudden surges of adrenaline.

It's important to spend time dwelling on this miracle. Don't make light of the fact that you're pregnant, and be sensitive regarding how you discuss your pregnancy. Many couples struggle with infertility and spend thousands of dollars trying to get into your shoes.

Celebrate the fact that the two of you have conceived. God has seen fit to grant to you a new addition to your family.

contractions

Contractions are initiated in the muscles of the cervix (neck of the uterus) and will become more frequent and intense as the actual delivery approaches. Mom may experience periodic tightening called Braxton-Hicks contractions at any time during the last few weeks of pregnancy, which precede the more intense and final contractions. Upon arrival at the maternity ward, it's not unusual to be sent back home for a time if it is deemed necessary. Help Mom time her contractions with the second hand of a watch so they can be reported to a doctor if requested.

cradle cap

Sometimes a flaky, white, patchy rash will appear on a newborn's scalp. You can gently remove this with a warm washcloth or fine-tooth comb and by washing Baby's head with a mild baby shampoo every few days. You may need to put a humidifier in the baby's room in the winter when central heating dries the air. You can also rub a couple of drops of baby oil into the crusty areas. Fifty percent of all babies get cradle cap in their first few months.

crib (*see also* SIDS)

The surroundings in which Baby sleeps need to be completely safe. Be careful using older models of cribs. New safety regulations are now in effect requiring that slats be no more than 2⅜ inches apart. Visit a baby or maternity store and talk with someone who is knowledgeable about baby furniture. Also, check to see that Baby's furniture is sturdy and won't fall over. Don't put a crib near a fireplace, a window, or in a drafty area. Realize that you may be reaching down into the crib several times per day to pick up Baby, and the height of the crib becomes more important as Baby gets bigger, because you can hurt your back bending over to pick up a heavier child. Once your baby can stand or climb out of the crib, it's time to move up to a toddler bed.

croup cough

Croup is a viral infection that causes swelling of the windpipe just below the vocal cords. If your baby's cough sounds like a bark and you hear wheezing, more than likely your baby has croup. This malady occurs more often in males and is most common between the ages of three months and three years. Croup usually hits in the winter months and is worse at night than during the day. Treatments include a cool mist humidifier or steam vaporizer in the child's room. Take your child into the bathroom to breathe the steam from a hot shower. Gently comforting and rocking your child relieves anxiety and helps ease breathing difficulties. If it's cold outside, you can also wrap your child in a blanket and sit outside for a few minutes.

If your baby's lips become blue or his breathing becomes labored, you will need to take your baby to the emergency room. Immediate action is especially necessary with infants because their airways are so small.

Each Christmas, we enjoyed bringing a living tree into our small home for the holidays. However, every Christmas one of our sons developed croup cough. We spent countless hours sitting on the frozen front porch trying to allow the cold air to open up his swollen airway. It was not until much later that we learned this same child was allergic to cedar and pine! We had inadvertently brought his allergen into the middle of our living room every year.

crowning

Moments before delivery, the top (crown) of the baby's head will appear protruding from the vagina. This is the moment, Dad, when your heart pounds like a bass drum. Your baby is leaving its pristine environment and entering into a whole new world. No wonder it's called crowning. This is the moment of moments. This is nine months or more of waiting, wrapped up into a nanosecond. Everyone's breath is held. Time freezes. More than likely, Mom is looking at you. You are looking at Baby. A thousand thoughts race through your head. Put down this book right now and rehearse it in your mind's eye. You will want to be physically, emotionally, and mentally present during these amazing moments.

crying (*see also* blues, colic, postpartum depression)

It's normal for a baby to cry. Form a checklist in your mind whenever your baby is crying. Is Baby wet? Hungry? Too hot or too cold? Teething? Does Baby need to burp? After going through this list, you can usually spot the problem. For a new dad, a crying baby can create one of the most frustrating experiences you've ever gone through. Remember, a good, long cry doesn't hurt your baby. You can try taking your baby on a walk, bathing him or her, wrapping Baby snugly in a blanket, or singing to Baby.

Never shake a baby. This can cause severe neck or permanent brain damage. Never toss or drop your baby. This will only make things worse. After reading those words, you may be thinking, "Oh, come on, I would never do that!" But until you have sat with a crying baby whom you are unable to calm, you can't fully understand how frustrating the experience can be. Believe us; a crying baby develops real patience in a person. If you feel deep anger or the desire to harm your infant in any way, call for help immediately. God is building patience and character in you through all the experiences you are going through as a new dad.

Moms sometimes cry too. Ten to twenty percent of mothers face some level of postpartum depression. Most cases are mild and can be treated with counseling and medicine, but some cases can deteriorate into delusions or even psychosis.

Crying in the Middle of the Night
Joe Bucha

Learning we were pregnant came as a bit of a surprise. Emily and I had been married only a little more than a year. Our plan was to wait at least three years before beginning our family, but obviously God's plan was on a different schedule. We were simultaneously shocked, overwhelmed, and excited. We eagerly attended childbirth classes, and our excitement and anticipation grew as we prepared for our child's arrival. Although the classes were of great help in what to expect as far as the delivery and birth of our child, we realized that neither of us had much experience with babies and the care of them.

One thing I became convinced of (for maybe the wrong reasons) was the need to breastfeed our son, Seth. I liked all of the health reasons and benefits of breastfeeding, but to be honest, the most attractive reason was that Emily would be the one to get up in the middle of the night for the feedings. We lived in a modest one-bedroom apartment and had the crib set up beside our bed so Emily could easily give Seth his nightly feedings.

Seth was very regular in reminding us when it was time to eat. The first few nights were tender, as Seth would squeak and cry to be fed. But as the weeks went on, the squeaks became squalls and the crying turned into wailing. Not only did Seth wake me up from a dead sleep, but what was initially a tender moment of feeding became a loud sucking and squirming and was rather irritating. Whether through sleep deprivation or just my selfishness coming to the surface, I blurted out, "I can't sleep with all of this noise! Can you take him into the living room to feed him so I can get some sleep?" Needless to say, we worked through some conflict and compromise in the caregiving for our son.

Emily also breastfed our other three children, and they too were loud in the middle of the night. But through the years, we learned to share various responsibilities. Emily got up to feed the kids, but you know those frequent "baby diaper explosions"? That's when I became "Captain Dad"!

Joe Bucha is a licensed professional counselor in Athens, Georgia.

D

Dad

This is your new name. This is what everyone will begin calling you. For example, a nurse may call out, "Dad, can you stand over here?" Or "Someone, go and get Dad; these contractions are getting more intense!" Get used to hearing this new moniker. The first time you hear it, you'll probably look over your shoulder. Wear this new name with pride. You're helping to raise a new member of the human race. You'll help to shape and mold a little person who will impact society. You're an impact player; you are da man—you are *Dad!*

And once you step into the role of father, it will dawn on you how much your heavenly Father loves you. You probably already know God loves you, but many new dads begin to genuinely feel God's unconditional love for them for the first time because of their own intense love for their new child.

date night

Establish a regular pattern of taking your wife out without the baby. If possible, enlist family or friends to watch the baby as the two of you enjoy an evening away. This date night will ease the frustration that comes when routine sets in. Movie theaters don't invite crying babies; nice restaurants aren't very accommodating either. But there are times when you simply must take a physical and mental break from the twenty-four-hour-a-day assignment of caring for your newborn. After a healthy break, you'll be more eager to get back to your baby. Schedule a date night and put it on the calendar.

d-day

Otherwise known as delivery day. Begin now to order your life around this day. Have you scheduled time away from work? Have you purchased and installed your infant car seat? The excitement builds as d-day approaches. In the moments leading up to d-day, you'll want to use a cell phone to remain in constant communication with Mom. Although your doctor has set a due date, babies have their own internal clocks. They may come a week or two early. They may arrive a few days late. They often decide to appear in the middle of the night. Whatever the case, d-day is inevitable, so plan ahead. Remember, it wasn't raining yet when Noah began building the ark.

dehydration

Your infant should produce six to eight wet diapers a day. If Baby has a dry mouth, a sunken soft spot, is acting lethargic, or is not wetting six to eight diapers a day, you should immediately consult your pediatrician. A baby can become dehydrated in less than twenty-four hours. Summer sun and warm environments can also induce dehydration. Always be mindful of your baby's fluid intake.

diaper bag

Never go anywhere with your baby without taking the diaper bag. Note Pettit's Law for Dads and Diapers: "The intensity of your baby's bowel movement is in direct proportion to the chances that you forget to bring the diaper bag." In other words, if you're thinking, "Oh, I'm just running a quick errand; surely I'll be alright for a few minutes," then you're headed for a diaper disaster. You'll have a mess on your hands, sleeves, car seat, shoes, and shirt. To repeat—never leave the house with your baby without bringing at least one diaper and a handful of wet wipes. Babies sense when you are "unarmed." A direct signal is sent from their eyes to their intestines. The first time you break Pettit's law, you'll remember with regret reading this warning. Dad, trust us on this one—this piece of advice alone was worth the price of this book.

Your diaper bag should include the basics: diaper, wet wipes, extra set of clothes, and bottle. You can also include a play toy, an extra blanket, medication, a picture book, or any other related item. You and this bag will become good friends as you haul it all over town. Since it will be accompanying Baby to the doctor's office and church nursery, make sure it includes proper identification. You wouldn't want another baby taking your own child's medicine, or vice versa.

diaper rash

Your baby will no doubt get diaper rash. This does not mean that you're a bad parent or have neglected your duties. It's important, though, to quickly take steps to alleviate the discomfort. The acidity in your baby's urine will sting and burn the red, patchy, affected areas. Liberally apply a diaper rash medicine several times per day. If Baby is allowed to spend time in a wet or soiled diaper, the condition will only become worse, so check Baby's diaper frequently and change dirty diapers immediately. If the rash refuses to disappear, consult your physician.

diapers

Have you had the debate yet about whether to go with disposable or cloth diapers? Some feel cloth diapers are cheaper and environmentally safer. Others say all the soap and water used in washing them offsets the environmental advantage. All agree that disposable diapers are more convenient.

Most public places of business have become aware that dads change diapers too. Many men's restrooms now provide changing tables that unfold from the wall. Try changing a baby's diaper on the floor. Yuck! Remember to dispose of diapers properly and quickly. Try several different diaper styles to see which works well for you. There are now swimming diapers as well for trips to the pool.

diarrhea (*see also* dehydration, stool)

Sooner or later, your baby will experience diarrhea. Treat it with extreme caution. Babies can become dehydrated quickly. You must replenish the lost fluids. Always consult your pediatrician when your infant develops diarrhea. There are some fluid replacement products on the market the doctor might recommend. If your wife is breastfeeding, she may be eating foods that do not agree with the baby's digestion. Or you may need to change formulas. If your infant begins to teethe early, swallowing the resulting excessive saliva may also be a cause.

dilation

In the hours leading to delivery, your doctor will use the term *dilation* to describe how many centimeters the cervix has opened. Dilation is measured in one to ten centimeter increments, with ten being the final stage where the cervix is completely open and ready for delivery. Your wife's cervix may be fairly well dilated in the days leading up to delivery.

doctor's appointments

Dad, it's important that you attend as many ob-gyn appointments as you can. You will surely want to be present when your baby appears on the sonogram screen for the first time or when it's possible for the first time to hear the heartbeat. Helping your wife get to these appointments shows her you care and that you plan on being a big help before, during, and after the baby is born. You will want to develop a rapport with the doctor as well, since he or she will be attending during the delivery. Parental involvement begins long before the baby appears on the scene.

due date

A verse in the Bible says, "Let us encourage one another—and all the more as you see the Day approaching" (Heb. 10:25). Although this verse is speaking of our Lord's return, apply it to your situation. As the due date approaches, your wife will begin to feel uncomfortable. She will feel big and bloated. None of her clothes will fit well. She will have trouble sleeping. She will need to urinate frequently. She will begin to mutter, "I can't wait to get this baby out of me!" This is where your encouraging words will be such a help. Now is the time for you to paint a picture of the future. "It won't be long now, honey . . . Just think, when this is all over we'll have a cute little baby . . . You look good pregnant . . . Can I get you anything? . . . Let me rub your back with lotion." These are all phrases you must not only master but carry out. Remember, all due dates are approximations. Don't fall apart if you are a few days early or late. Most doctors will not, however, allow you to go more than two weeks past your due date.

E

emergencies

It's important to be prepared in case an emergency should occur either before or after the delivery. Before the delivery, you should be in possession of the phone numbers where your ob-gyn can be reached. You should also have the phone numbers and schedules of those one or two people who are going to be assisting you with any last-minute details. Have all this information written down and displayed in a prominent place. You should also know the driving route to the hospital and the location of the maternity entrance. Many hospitals now register maternity patients ahead of time so that when the moment comes, moms can be quickly checked into a labor and recovery room. At any time during the ninth month, you should be on an "on-call" basis with friends, family, and work. "Sure I'll be there, unless we have our baby that day," is a helpful way to remind others of your current status.

Once you bring your baby home, many additional phone numbers should be displayed in a prominent place: fire, police, ambulance, pediatrician, poison control, and the hospital closest to your home. Also put this list of numbers in your wallet or cell phone. Will you know where your child's records are? Will you take your child to an Ident-a-Kid program to be registered in case of some disaster? These are all situations none of us like to think about, but as a good dad, you'll want to be prepared. And don't forget to store some of these important numbers in your cell phone under the contact name ICE, which stands for "In Case of Emergency."

emotions

Your feelings have more than likely been bungee jumping lately. Sometimes you can't wait to see and hold your baby. At other times it all seems like a dream. And you may have even wished the baby would just go away. Remember, these are all normal emotions. Just like God allows your baby nine months to develop physically in the womb, you have nine months to develop emotionally. Having a baby will bring a greater maturity into certain areas of your life. When you're scheduled to pick up your baby at a certain time, you simply must be there. Babies don't sit at the bus stop by themselves waiting for you. In the same way that lifting weights helps you become physically stronger, caring for your baby helps you become emotionally stronger. You may find, for example, that assignments at work you once shied away from now seem less challenging in comparison to quieting a fussy baby. You'll be drawn to men who have children and seek them out for advice. Don't let your emotions overwhelm you. Difficult moments that seem insurmountable at the time will diminish as your baby grows.

environment

To a large degree you have the right to establish the environment in the delivery and recovery room. What music, if any, do you want playing? Do you want the television on? Will you want flowers or balloons? Can other people come into the room to visit? Can visitors bring children? What mood do you want to set? Some nurses are more reserved while others "take charge." If you don't feel comfortable with something, speak up. Nurses and doctors cannot read your mind or know what your wishes are until you verbalize them.

epidural

An epidural block is a kind of regional analgesic. An anesthesiologist or nurse-anesthetist injects the anesthetic into the space just outside the *dura*—the sac membrane that surrounds the spine. Your wife will lie curled on her side or will sit on the edge of the bed for the injection. The anesthetist passes a catheter—a very thin, flexible, hollow tube—through the needle, then withdraws the needle and tapes the catheter in place so he can add medication through it as needed. That some women choose this method while others don't doesn't mean that some are stronger or weaker than others. In fact, most women today choose some form of medication. According to one survey, more than 75 percent of women reported that they received an epidural, including 71 percent of women who had a vaginal birth (Eugene R. Declercq, Carol Sakala, Maureen P. Corry, and Sandra Applebaum, "Listening to Mothers II: Report of the Second National U.S. Survey of Women's Childbearing Experiences: Conducted January–February 2006," *Journal of Perinatal Education* 16, no. 4 [Fall 2007], 15–17). Again, as with other medical procedures surrounding the birth event, people hold strong opinions on the topic of epidurals. Talk with many different moms so that you can make an informed decision—then stick to your guns.

episiotomy

An episiotomy is a surgical cut in the perineum, the muscular area between the vagina and the anus, and it's often done using a local anesthetic. Although an episiotomy doesn't have to be a routine part of labor, your medical attendants may perform one to speed delivery and prevent your wife's vagina from tearing as your baby is born. Many doctors believe the planned incision of an episiotomy heals more easily than the tears that can happen spontaneously during delivery. Discuss all of these labor-pain-relief issues with your doctor well ahead of your due date. There's a reason they call it labor!

extended family (*see also* grandparents)

Whatever underlying tensions you presently experience with your family, including relationships with your wife's family, they will most likely come to a peak during the days leading up to the delivery. Who will be in the delivery room with you? Who will be present at the hospital? Can family come and visit whenever they want or do you want them to call ahead first? Will you use a family name in the baby's name? Believe it or not, matters concerning extended family can become a headache if clear boundaries are not established ahead of time. Since Pam works in a hospital delivery room, she has seen some of the problems "up close and personal." Some relatives feel they have a right to know each and every detail. Others are offended if they are not the first to know exactly what is happening. Some new moms make the mistake of spending all of their precious time on the phone, retelling the events of the delivery. Others allow visitors to parade in and out, leaving no private time for Mom, Dad, and Baby. You get the picture; set limits on interruptions. This is a time for your new family to spend together. There'll be plenty of opportunities for visitors and stories in the months ahead.

··

First-Time Father
Keith Rose

My wife, Brenda, and I were more than excited about our new baby. We considered our pregnancy as a generous gift from God, because we had thought we might not be able to have a child. Now, as I looked at Brenda in her eighth month, there was no doubt she was pregnant and getting ready to deliver—soon! (By the way, just when you think your wife can't possibly get larger . . . you'll be surprised by what the ninth month brings.)

As d-day approached, we packed our suitcase for the hospital and got everything ready. God has blessed me with Brenda and her organized approach to life. All was set. We had read books, gone to delivery classes, prayed, and now we'd even packed. We were ready!

It was the ninth month, and now Brenda was really amazing! It was getting a bit tough for her to maneuver, given her cute belly, but her energy was back. She was ready for delivery—but the baby didn't seem to want to come. So Brenda hit the treadmill and walked, hoping to stimulate labor. We also needed to pick up some carpeting for the baby's room, so Brenda volunteered to help carry it from the warehouse and up the stairs. I'm convinced it was the carpet toting that brought on her labor. That night, Brenda told me it was time to go to the hospital.

I'm a very calm person—normally. But when Brenda said, "We need to go to the hospital," something came unglued in the back of my head. Don't be surprised when the same thing happens to you. The next thing I remember is being at the hospital. I don't recall driving at all. By the time we got settled into the delivery room, I realized I had completely forgotten the suitcase. It was God's way of preparing me for what was to come. Because, despite all the planning and preparation, you'll never really be ready—and, you'll lean on God even more.

The nurse said we had plenty of time. So I glued my head back on, rushed home for the suitcase (while Brenda got settled in), and returned to help for the big event.

Two suggestions for the time when you're actually in the delivery room:

1. Be a companion, not a coach. Brenda needed to squeeze my arm; she didn't need me to tell her to "breathe" and "push."

2. Keep your eyes open. Although we had some of the best health care in the world, medical staffs are made up of people like you and me—and they're not perfect. At one point, Brenda's blood pressure fell so low that she was almost in shock. It looked like she was sleeping, but the digital number on the monitor kept getting lower and lower, so I went out and asked the nurse if that was normal. She looked scared and ran into the room with several other nurses to revive Brenda. Praise God, all went well with the delivery.

The delivery is a life-changing event. When I saw the face of my newborn daughter, Adelle, for the first time . . . love is a word that doesn't seem strong enough. That love will grow and sustain you as you morph into your new role as a dad. It will also help you through the first diaper change. Don't worry, you'll get better at it after three hundred or more diapers.

Fast forward a few years . . .

We just had our third girl, Olivia. I fell in love all over again. What incredible gifts! Adelle is now six, Brianna is four, and now we have Olivia. A friend told me to cherish every moment, because children grow up in the blink of an eye. It's true.

As a new dad, you'll be exhausted, amazed, and stretched. But you're also accepting one of the greatest gifts God has for you—the gift of a new life.

Keith Rose is a marketing specialist in Danville, California.

F

fatigue

We know what some of you are thinking: "How hard can it be to take care of a newborn?" An experiment was carried out where an Olympic-class athlete was asked to follow a one-year-old baby around for an entire day. Mimicking the infant's every move was the objective. If the baby rolled over, the athlete rolled over. If the baby crawled around the room, the athlete got down on hands and knees and crawled around the room. Guess what the results were? After only three hours, the athlete was exhausted. And the baby? The baby was laughing. The mother noted that the baby was, in fact, enjoying himself as much as at any other time in his short existence.

Babies seem to have boundless energy. They will get into your sock drawer and drop them out one by one. They will unroll an entire roll of toilet paper, spreading it all around the bathroom. If you turn your head for a moment, they may crawl into the next county. This brings us to the "fatigue factor." You and your wife need to get some help. You need to schedule a caregiver or babysitter on a regular basis. You may think you can't afford to. We say you can't afford not to. If you are angry or tired all the time, Dad, you are of little help to your wife or baby. When fatigue sets in—and it will—find a time and place for you and Mom to refuel. She and Baby will thank you.

Remember the sage advice: "If Mama ain't happy, ain't nooooobody happy." And, happy wife . . . happy life!

fear

An emotion most men admit to experiencing in the delivery room is fear. There are many things that can and sometimes do go wrong. It's important to dwell on the positive in the delivery room. You've selected a competent physician who has assisted in hundreds of deliveries. You're working with a team of nurses and aides who want the very best for both you and your baby. Family and friends are praying for a safe delivery. Your wife is going to do all she can to bring Baby into the world. Focus on all of these things and cast fear aside. This is the time for you to be strong and courageous! Even if problems arise, you'll need to stand by your wife's side and take on together whatever complications come at you. "For God has not given us a spirit of timidity [fear], but of power and love and discipline" (2 Tim. 1:7 NASB). Isn't that a wonderful promise to take into the delivery room? There is nothing wrong with experiencing fear; however, we should not let it debilitate us, especially during the critical moments surrounding the delivery. Courage is defined as acting boldly in spite of fear.

feeding

Have you seen the cute television commercials where Baby throws food back at Dad? Or the one where Baby gets more food on himself and his high chair than in his mouth? When it happens to you, it's not funny. Feeding an infant takes time and patience. It's always best to set up a routine. Try to seat the baby in the same area for each feeding. Put the bib on the baby. Have the washcloth ready. Vegetables before fruits. (Why? Because normally, when babies eat something sweet, like fruits, they then don't want to go back to something like turkey spread.) Before long, Baby will begin grabbing at the spoon. He or she is not being defiant, just curious. Besides, you wouldn't want to still be spoon-feeding your baby at age five, would you? It's normal for babies to want to feed themselves. Just be ready. After a good feeding, your wife can bathe your baby and you can go take a shower. Sometimes dads will eat a large meal while giving their own baby just a few bites. Then, since the dad is so full, they may think, "Man, we're stuffed," when only the dad is filled and the baby is still hungry. While a dad eats three square meals a day, a new baby needs to eat every three or four hours. Don't be guilty of confusing the two appetites.

fertility (*see also* conception, infertility)

Fertility involves the ability to conceive. It is estimated that during intercourse, approximately 300 million sperm are discharged at each ejaculation. Only one, however, remains alive through the entire process of fertilization, and even that happens only occasionally. Never be blasé that you and your wife have conceived. Rejoice that you are going to have a baby, but be sensitive to other couples who can't conceive. We had two children very quickly after we were married. Sometimes we made jokes about how easy it was for us to conceive. Later we had couples talk to us and share the pain of infertility: "We've been trying to get pregnant for four years . . ." So exercise caution if you joke around about getting pregnant simply by holding hands or kissing, as there are couples in your social circles who would give almost anything to be in your shoes. Fertility and conception are amazing processes from God. Don't take them lightly.

fever

The body has an amazing ability to regulate and control its own temperature. But sometimes things get out of control. Here are guidelines for knowing when to call your doctor. If your baby has a temperature above 101, is crying inconsolably, is difficult to awaken, is confused or delirious, has had a seizure, has a stiff neck, has purple spots on the skin, has difficulty breathing and does not feel better after nose is cleared, or is acting very sick, immediately consult your pediatrician. Here are two other guidelines: if a low-grade fever is present for more than forty-eight hours, or if a fever goes away for twenty-four hours and then returns, immediately contact your pediatrician. Dad, don't mess with a fever. It's your baby's way of telling you something isn't right. Learn how to use a digital thermometer or temporal scanner. And don't hesitate to take your baby's temperature early and often when you even suspect they might be ill. Better safe than sorry.

fitness

Developing strong muscle tone and skin elasticity will help your wife during the delivery. Together, you and your wife can do simple exercises to strengthen the legs, back, and pelvic areas. Working these muscles will help later on during delivery. Walking and swimming are also good ways to stay fit during pregnancy. Bicycling and high-impact aerobics are not recommended for pregnant women. As always, check with your ob-gyn before beginning any strenuous exercise programs. No doubt your wife has put on weight. Help her out by avoiding all-you-can-eat buffets or ordering dinner-for-two specials. As her belly expands, she will need to eat several small meals a day and take walks to suppress the gas and stomachaches.

While we're on this topic we want to say a word about a new fad that has popped up in certain circles. Some women are trying to get their body into "aerobics instructor" fitness shape only days after delivery. This is not only unrealistic but can be dangerous. Mom's body has just been through a grueling nine-month odyssey. It is highly improbably that she will be in supermodel shape only three or four days after delivery. Set up a fitness plan in the weeks, not days, after delivery.

flowers

Guys, this one is a no-brainer. Purchase flowers for your wife during the time she is in the maternity room. Many things can go wrong in a delivery. The delivery of your flowers should not be one of them. A little planning is in order. In the moments after delivery, you will be pulled in every direction. Nurses will be coming and going. Family members whom you have never met will be appearing out of the woodwork. Coworkers will drop by. And, since you've read this book, you will quietly slip away and use your cell phone and make the order. Buy according to budget. Your wife has just gone through nine long months of tolerating crazy hormones and watching her body change. She has just been through the painful process of delivery. For goodness sake, buy your woman some flowers! If you don't, you'll be reminded of this omission during the child's high school graduation. As your daughter walks across the platform to receive her diploma, you will comment, "We did it, honey! We raised her well, didn't we?" But your wife will remind you, "Yeah, honey, the only thing missing was *flowers in the maternity room!*"

football hold

The first time you hold your baby, you'll probably feel uncomfortable or awkward. You know you should support the neck and head because your baby is not yet strong enough to hold up their head on their own and is flopping around like a wet fish. Try the football hold. Place the head in the inside bend of your arm. Lay the body down your arm, and secure the baby with your free hand. In other words, hold the baby like you would a football. Now you look like an old pro as you walk through the hospital smiling with your newborn. Let the video roll and the cameras flash—you're a new dad! However, don't try to get cute. Babies can arch their back, fidget, and squirm out of your arms. Always practice extra caution while holding your baby. It is not a great idea to try to toss your baby high into the air or balance them over your head with one hand just to wow a group of friends.

forceps (*see also* cesarean section, vacuum extraction)
If during the later stages of labor there is "failure to progress," your delivery doctor may advise the use of forceps. These are metal tongs that help the baby's head move through the last stages of the birth canal. They can cause bruises on the shoulders, cheeks, and face, but they may become a lifesaver. Don't hesitate to give your consent to their use. If forceps or vacuum extraction doesn't move things along, your doctor will most likely consider the next step: performing a C-section.

formula (*see also* bottle-feeding)
Most newborns should eat every three to four hours. Babies do not require cereal, juice, or baby food until they are four to six months or older. Your pediatrician will help you know when your baby is ready for these. Here are some hints concerning formulas. You can use ordinary tap water to mix with formula; the water does not have to be boiled. Formulas come in powder, concentrated liquid, or pre-mixed containers. Always read the container to make sure you're mixing correctly. After the formula is mixed and refrigerated, it is usable for up to twenty-four hours. Throw away any formula that is older than twenty-four hours. After the feeding, dispose of formula that Baby does not eat. Don't put it back in the refrigerator as it could make the baby sick. And, finally, do not feed the baby from a bottle that has been sitting out for an hour or more.

fraternity of fathers
Welcome to the group! You are now among the cadre of men who have been blessed with a child. When you pass another dad at the mall who has a couple of kids in tow, you may receive a nod that says, "I know what you're going through." You may catch yourself sitting around at a party swapping diaper horror stories or cross-country travel tales. You may suddenly brag to a friend, "Ah, that's nothing,

man. You ran a marathon, but one time I watched our newborn for three days while Pam was out of town!"

frozen breast milk (*see also* breastfeeding)

If your wife works outside of the home on a regular basis, she may elect to use a breast pump. If this is the case, you'll be refrigerating and warming breast milk. After your wife expresses herself with the breast pump, follow these guidelines: Place the milk in a clean container. Mark the container with the date and time. Freeze the breast milk immediately; it is good in the freezer for up to six months. Warm the frozen milk in a container of hot water until it is room temperature. If your wife does elect to use a breast pump, encourage her often. It is difficult for a marketplace mom to find times and places to express her milk. She needs your encouragement, not funny remarks, during this time.

frustration

You've probably picked up on this recurring theme in our book by now: Taking care of a newborn can be downright frustrating. Don't get us wrong—there are times of incredible bliss. You'll experience the highest of highs while caring for your newborn. There'll be moments when, as your baby is falling asleep in your arms, your attention focuses on a tiny finger or curled eyelash. You will cherish the moment when your infant first says "Dada" or takes a first step. But we'd be remiss if we didn't prepare you for the downsides, because as with all mountaintop experiences, there are times when you must visit the valley.

You may be up in the middle of the night with a sick baby, knowing you have a crucial presentation to make at work in a few hours. You may accidentally set your baby down on your computer keyboard and delete three days' worth of work. Your baby may crawl into the bathroom and drop your tie into the toilet. Or your baby may spit up on the third clean outfit you've put on her or him while trying to get to an important appointment on time. Know that it's normal to feel real frustration at times. "I wish we would've never had this monster," may be a phrase that enters your mind. These are normal thoughts and are to be expected. All new dads experience heightened periods of exasperation.

If you feel deep, dark depression, however, or experience feelings of wanting to hurt or harm your child in any way, you need to seek help. You need intervention, someone who can relieve you on a regular basis. You need a breath of fresh air. Step back and take the long view of what you're trying to accomplish. You're not raising a baby; you're raising an adult. The project will take many years. Don't let unchecked low levels of frustration simmer in the psyche for long periods of time, in either you or your wife. Both of you need breaks.

fussy

Learn to discern the differences in your baby's numerous kinds of cries. All babies are fussy at times, but it helps to remember that at this early stage, crying is the only way your baby can communicate with you. If Baby could speak plainly, he or she might announce, "Hey you! Yeah, you over there. Can you please come and change this wet diaper?" or "Can I get some milk already? It's an hour past feeding time, you know!" Since your baby can't yet plainly articulate needs, he or she resorts to crying, the only language your baby knows. He or she may be fussy for simple reasons: wet, hungry, tired, or cold. Or, more importantly, the baby may be hurting or ill. In other words, you as a dad must be sensitive to the needs of your baby.

You may be used to working in an environment where you solve problems all day long. But working with a newborn is a new kind of problem. You won't be able to walk away from your baby or pass Baby off to an associate. You may become amazed at how your wife can settle your baby down so quickly while when you try it, you and the baby grow more and more frustrated. Babies are very young and small but very smart and completely aware of their surroundings. They can smell that you are not Mom, they can feel the tension in your arm muscles, and they seem to have a sixth sense that you don't yet fully know what you're doing. Over time, your baby will adapt wonderfully to you *if you work at it.* If you never take the time and energy to bond with your baby, he or she will have a harder time becoming comfortable with you.

My Dad
Chuck Swindoll

My dad died last night. He left like he had lived. Quietly. Graciously. With dignity. Without demands or harsh words or even a frown, he surrendered himself—a tired, frail, humble gentleman—into the waiting arms of his Savior. Death, selfish and cursed enemy of man, won another battle.

As I stroked the hair from his forehead and kissed him good-bye, a hundred boyhood memories played around in my head.

- When I learned to ride a bike, he was there.
- When I wrestled with the multiplication table, his quick wit erased the hassle.
- When I discovered the adventure of driving a car, he was near, encouraging me.
- When I got my first job (delivering newspapers), he informed me how to increase my subscriptions and win the prize. It worked!
- When I mentioned a young woman I had fallen in love with, he pulled me aside and talked straight about being responsible for her welfare and happiness.

· When I did a hitch in the Marine Corps, the
discipline I had learned from him made the
transition easier.

From him I learned to seine for shrimp. How to gig
flounder and catch trout and red fish. How to open oyster
shells and fix crab gumbo and chili . . . and popcorn . . .
and make rafts out of old inner tubes and gunny sacks.
I was continually amazed at his ability to do things like
tie fragile mantles on the old Coleman lantern, keep a fire
going in the rain, play the harmonica with his hands behind
his back, and keep three strong-willed kids from tearing the
house down.

Last night I realized I had him to thank for my deep love
for America. And for knowing how to tenderly care for my
wife. And for laughing at impossibilities. And for some of
the habits I have picked up, like approaching people with
a positive spirit rather than a negative one, staying with a
task until it is finished, taking good care of my personal
belongings, keeping my shoes shined, speaking up rather
than mumbling, respecting authority, and standing alone
(if necessary) in support of my personal convictions rather
than giving in to more popular opinions. For these things I
am deeply indebted to the man who raised me.

Certain smells and sounds now instantly remind me of
my dad. Oyster stew. The ocean breeze. Smoke from an
expensive cigar. The nostalgic whine of a harmonica. A
camping lantern and white gas. Car polish. Fun songs from
the 30s and 40s. Freshly mowed grass. A shrill whistle from
a father to his kids around supper time. And Old Spice after
shave.

Because a father impacts his family so permanently, I
think I understand better than ever what the Scripture means
when Paul wrote:

Having so fond an affection for you, we were well-pleased to impart to you not only the gospel of God but also our own lives, because you had become very dear to us. . . . Just as you know how we were exhorting and encouraging and imploring each one of you as a father would his own children, so that you may walk in a manner worthy of the God who calls you into His own kingdom and glory. (1 Thessalonians 2:8, 11–12 NASB)

Admittedly, much of my dad's instruction was indirect—by model rather than by explicit statement. I do not recall his overt declarations of love as clearly as I do his demonstrations of it. His life revolved around my mother, the darling and delight of his life. Of that I am sure. When she left over nine years ago, something of him died as well. And so—to her he has been joined and they are, together, with our Lord. In the closest possible companionship one can imagine.

In this my sister, my brother, and I find our greatest comfort—they are now forever with the Lord eternally freed from pain and aging and death. Secure in Jesus Christ our Lord. Absent from the body and at home with Him. And with each other.

Last night I said good-bye. I'm still trying to believe it. You'd think it would be easy, since his illness had persisted for more than three years. How well I remember the Sunday he suffered that first in a series of strokes as I was preaching. God granted him several more years to teach many of us to appreciate the things we tend to take for granted.

He leaves in his legacy a well-marked Bible I treasure, a series of feelings that I need to deepen my roots, and a thousand memories that comfort me as I replace denial with acceptance and praise.

I await heaven's gate opening in the not-too-distant future. So do other Christians, who anxiously await Christ's return. Most of them anticipate hearing the soft strum of a harp or the sharp, staccato blast of a trumpet. Not me. I will hear the nostalgic whine of a harmonica . . . held in the hands of the man who died last night . . . or did he? The memories are as fresh as this morning's sunrise.

Taken from Come Before Winter and Share My Hope *by Charles R. Swindoll. Copyright © 1985 by Charles R. Swindoll, Inc. Used by permission of Zondervan.*

Chuck Swindoll is the senior pastor of Stonebriar Community Church, Frisco, Texas, and is heard on the popular radio broadcast Insight for Living.

G

gender differences

People don't intentionally set out to call your cute little baby girl a boy or vice versa. But sometimes we don't have enough clues. Put a pink outfit on a girl or a blue jumper on a boy, and now we can tell. Put a pink bow in your baby girl's hair or a baseball outfit on your little guy, and we have signs. It's important, too—in order for your own child's gender development to become healthy and balanced—that both parents stay involved in everyday activities. You as the husband will need to diaper, bathe, bottle-feed, and rock your baby on a regular basis. The antiquated idea, "That is the mother's role," went out with rotary dial telephones. At eighteen months, your baby will already have a firm sense of his or her own gender. Isn't that amazing! Dads, Baby needs to feel the roughness of the whiskers on your face and the deeper tones of your voice on a daily basis. Your baby is differentiating between you and Mom all the time. Normally, your infant will "attach" emotionally with Mom at a very early stage. This bonding with you takes more time and effort. At the earliest stages, the only two people in Baby's world are "Mama" and "not Mama." As the days turn to weeks, however, you become a real player in your infant's world. Don't let these important days pass you by. Many of the new fathers we talk with think, "When my baby's older, then I'll get involved."

Your baby is reaching out to you *now*, so get involved, and stay involved—from day one. They grow and change so quickly. Try not to miss out on these special times. You never get these moments back.

Gerber baby

What every parent thinks their new child looks like. Someone will say, "What a cute baby. It looks just like the Gerber baby!" You'll answer, "Yeah, we know." All parents think their own baby is the cutest. If you don't believe us, just wait. You'll hear stories from other parents concerning offers to shoot magazine covers and television commercials. Remember, beauty is in the eye of the beholder, especially when it comes to babies. Looks change almost overnight. Skin rashes can develop, and fuzzy hair can stand straight up on picture day. Take comments about your baby's looks with a grain of salt. Some self-appointed prophet may announce, "Well, your baby didn't get good looks, so I bet he's going to be athletic," or a similar frivolous comment. When you encounter these people and their rude remarks, don't go into shock and drop your beautiful baby. All babies are special and unique in their own way. Try to avoid constant comparisons.

gestation

The medical community uses this term to describe how far along the baby has developed in the pregnancy. The normal amount of time for gestation is ten lunar months or forty weeks. So halfway through your pregnancy, your baby will be twenty weeks gestation. Your baby is viable outside of the womb at around twenty-three weeks, provided he or she receives intense medical care in a neonatal intensive care unit (NICU). Begin to count down the time toward your due date in weeks. When someone asks you, "How far along?" you can reply, "Only twelve more weeks to go."

While your baby is hidden from public view, safely tucked away in the perfect environment of your wife's uterus, getting nutrition via the placenta, know that "behind the scenes," much activity is taking place. Bones are growing, muscles are stretching, and specific sounds are being "recorded" in the developing brain. While your wife is bonding naturally with the baby, simply due to their close physical proximity, you'll need to be proactive during pregnancy and move toward your baby. Talk to your baby, gently rub your wife's tummy and announce, "I'm your daddy, and I can't wait to see you!" Experts tell us babies at very early stages of gestation can recognize sound, music, and even voice patterns.

glowing

Some women are extremely sick during the first trimester of their pregnancy. They may look and feel down. After this period, however, many report an increase in energy, feelings of happiness, and an increase in self-esteem. Someone may comment to your wife that she looks as if she is literally glowing. Her hair and skin may become clearer and softer. Her face may radiate warmth and kindness. Some men claim that when their wife was in this stage she "never looked more healthy." So when you hear someone announce that your wife is glowing, don't reach for a fire extinguisher.

grace

One of the character traits in which you will grow is grace. The word *grace* means unmerited favor. God will give you the grace to make it through one more night. Grace allows you to have patience with your changing situation. And now that you're a dad you need to show more grace to others. Do you show much grace toward your wife? Show even more now that she's also a mom. Be gracious to those who provide a helping hand with your new baby. Let grace reign as you learn to parent like your heavenly Father. All you have to offer is the legacy you leave behind. Leave a gracious one.

grandparents (*see also* extended family)

You may or may not be physically or emotionally close to your parents and in-laws. Either way, you are now entering into a new realm of relationship with them. They are now Grandma and Grandpa. This may be the first time they've worn this mantle, or they may be seasoned pros. Have you discussed with them your desires and goals? Do you want them to help watch the baby on a regular basis? Don't take their help for granted. Most grandparents today are very active. Many still work full-time. You will need to be sensitive to their needs and they to yours. Do you want them to purchase numerous gifts or just a few? Do you want them to call before they visit? Do you want them present in the delivery room? Will you decide to use a long-standing family name for your baby? You can see how you and your wife need to discuss these matters ahead of time. Work hard to keep the lines of communication open and clear with all extended family members.

growth spurt

At certain times, your newborn will want to eat and sleep more than usual. This is normal and to be expected. There are times when your baby's body will grow at an incredible, accelerated rate. That favorite outfit will be too tight, and at times you'll think you can actually see the baby growing right before your very eyes. Don't get too upset at sudden gains or losses. And whatever you do, don't get into the comparison game of sizing up your baby with others of similar age. Every baby is unique. Unless you see a rapid, unexpected weight loss (in which case, schedule an appointment with your pediatrician), don't measure your baby constantly with the neighbor's baby. Over time, one pound and one inch differences will become a passing memory.

heartburn

Heartburn is a common complaint of moms during pregnancy. The two biggest culprits are overeating and spicy foods. Your wife may not be overeating; it's just that the size of her stomach has been decreased because your baby is pushing up next to it. The best remedies are for her to avoid eating immediately before lying down; eat more frequent, smaller-proportioned meals; use pillows at bedtime; and ask your doctor about antacids. In addition, your wife needs to drink plenty of water.

hemorrhoids

Many moms experience hemorrhoids either before or after delivery. These are caused by extra pressure building up around the rectum, anus, and sphincter area during the pregnancy, as well as from the heavy pushing during labor. Some hemorrhoids are severe enough to require minor surgery, while other cases can be treated with an over-the-counter topical ointment.

hernia

Some infants may develop a hernia. This can happen when part of the intestinal tract protrudes through the stomach lining. There are various causes for this condition, but it can normally be corrected through minor surgery.

home business

Many expectant moms talk about returning to the marketplace right away after giving birth—until they hold their baby in their arms for the very first time. The bonding that develops between the mother and baby in just six to eight weeks can become so strong that it changes previous intentions. It's true that some women, for a variety of reasons, are prohibited from remaining at home on a full-time basis. With that said, however, we believe it is best if Mom can be with Baby as much as possible in the days and weeks following delivery. It may be that a home-based business or home-based work is a viable option. After calculating the numbers, you may find a way to avoid long hours of mother-child separation. Be sure to take into account the cost of travel, clothing, child care, meals, and so forth when you decide if Mom needs to work outside of the home. Many employers are now allowing mothers and, in some cases, fathers to take an extended leave of absence to care for a newborn. Check into it.

The Power Lunch
Paul Pettit

"Austin," I said, "one more thing . . . I'm glad you're my son." My oldest boy and I had just finished a recent lunchtime picnic and were saying good-bye to each other before heading back to our own day-to-day routines.

There's nothing more powerful in the life of your young son or daughter than memories cultivated during times of personal interaction. It's unfortunate that many parents today find these special moments occurring less and less frequently.

The problem results from both the type of work many of us now do and the speed at which technological advancements take place. During the pre-Industrial Age (think *Little House on the Prairie*), fathers and sons worked together on farms or side by side in a family-run business. Skills and traditions were handed down from generation to generation. Mothers taught daughters how to cook, sew, clean, care for newborns, and a host of other equally important skills. Fathers taught sons how to plow fields, plant crops, make tools, and run a business.

During the Industrial Revolution, however, many fathers left the farm or the family business to work in a large mill, factory, or warehouse. Sometimes fathers and sons continued working alongside each other, but most spent the workday apart, and this separation began a tearing of the family fabric which has not been repaired. With technological advances in the fields of travel, communication, and industry, many now ask what can be done to recover some of this lost time of personal interaction. Today, the typical family eats a quick breakfast—maybe—and is then catapulted into several different directions for the remainder of the day. What can be done to lessen the impact of our increasingly fragmented society?

The following revolutionary technique, employed on a regular basis, will help you buy back some of your lost family time. Are you ready? Regularly schedule a lunch with your son or daughter. I can already hear some of you asking, "That's it? What's so earth-shattering about that?" But think about it. When was the last time you sat down with your son or daughter—just the two of you—for a planned lunch? It won't happen unless you place it on the calendar. So schedule it much like you would an important high-level meeting—because it is.

Schedule this event about once every other month to keep it special. It helps if you eat in a quiet place where you can discuss events taking place at school or home. Why lunch? The problem with a breakfast appointment is the pace: it always seems rushed. A dinner meeting, on the other hand, normally takes place at the end of the day, when energy levels are waning and other events are already scheduled. I've found that lunchtime is the best opportunity to break into my child's world and discover what he or she is thinking. The excitement begins early in the morning when I announce, "Don't forget, I'm meeting you for lunch today." Then throughout the day, I find myself thinking about and looking forward to interacting with my son or daughter over a midday meal.

When I walk into our children's school to pick them up and they first catch a glimpse of me, they literally run and jump into my arms. (I assume the tradition will cease when they are sixteen years old, but I hope their hearts will still race a bit when we walk off to our regularly scheduled lunch date.)

During the middle of the day, children are normally engulfed in their own everyday affairs. I like to ask my sons and daughters questions like, "You guys all walked over here straight from music class. Is that your normal routine?" "Hey, look at those construction workers building that tall building. Would you like to do that when you grow up?" "That older lady over there looks like Grandma, doesn't she? What do you think Grandma is doing right this minute?" You get the point. The idea is to engage in meaningful conversation that will cultivate powerful feelings of love and attachment.

What if you work in a job that's not conducive to leaving the worksite? Making a lunch date is important enough that you arrange to have your child brought to you. I'm serious. There must be someone who would be willing to bring your child to your worksite. Trust me; it will be worth the effort.

When I am on my children's "turf," I find the questions normally flow from me to them. I ask them questions about their day and their surroundings. When the kids are on my turf, however, the questions flow in the opposite direction. My children ask me questions such as, "Is this computer yours? Can you play games on here?" "Where is that picture I made for you?" or "Which one of these people around here is your boss?"

Your child longs for your undivided attention. Do not bring a coworker or meet your child with a group of his or her peers. Meet with your child one-on-one. There is no emotional boost more powerful than your walking into your child's world and capturing a few powerful moments alone with him or her. The work back at the job can usually wait for an hour, but a lingering lunch with your son or daughter is a priceless moment that can never be recaptured.

Two high-level executives getting together for lunch is truly a powerful event. But for sheer impact, a planned lunch between a parent and child is the ultimate power lunch. Why not schedule one right now?

I

immunizations (*see also* well-baby checkups)

It's very important for your baby to receive all of the normal immunizations required. Some of these will take place shortly after delivery. Most of them, however, will take place during well-baby checkups in your pediatrician's office over the period of the first two years. Be sure to keep accurate, up-to-date records of these shots. Over the coming years, you will need these shot records for many different reasons: school, summer camp, sports teams, accidents, doctor's visits, and many others.

infertility

Twenty-five percent of all couples in the United States struggle with infertility. A couple can be considered infertile if they have been trying to conceive for more than twelve months without a pregnancy. Why are we raising this issue when you are going to be a dad? Because many other couples struggle with infertility, and you will more than likely be sharing your good news with such a couple. Since they have been unable to conceive, they may not be as excited as you are. So we urge you to be extra sensitive with your joy and exuberance. Many couples who struggle with infertility may be facing depression, anxiety, and anger. Imagine their feelings and emotional struggle when month after month they see no sign of conception. And then, in a moment of carelessness, you may announce, "I can't believe we're pregnant already. We were hoping to wait awhile!" or "Oh, brother, we were just starting to save some money, and now we come up pregnant." You get the idea. Be alert to other couples who are hurting in this area.

intercourse

After conception, many men fear that resuming intercourse will harm the baby or somehow hurt Mom. You must discuss with your wife her feelings regarding physical intimacy. Some women feel an even greater desire for cuddling and kissing during pregnancy. Others feel ill much of the time and simply don't want you to touch them. The slightest whiff of your favorite cologne can send her running for the nearest bathroom to hug the porcelain throne. Once you find what is comfortable, know that sex with your wife will not harm the developing fetus. You will need to be more sensitive. And, since her body is rapidly changing, you may want to experiment with new positions.

After delivery, your wife's libido and vaginal secretions will be diminished due to hormone depletion. This can cause painful intercourse. Also, after the delivery, doctors advise that couples refrain from sex for six weeks. We recently heard of one new dad who, upon hearing this injunction from his doctor, asked incredulously, "I'm sorry, Doc, I thought I heard you say no sex for six weeks!" That's right, Dad—start taking long runs and cold showers. You're becoming a more intense servant-leader, and a huge part of being a good dad is learning more and more to act in selfless ways.

J

jaundice

See bilirubin.

juices

Most nutritionists agree that a baby does not need juices until he or she is able to drink from a cup. Most juices are considered empty calories that take the place of nutritious breast milk or formula. Rest assured, formula or breast milk is all your baby needs nutritionally for the first year of life. Sugary juices can relieve an infant's hunger. . . for a short time. But they will not satisfy true hunger pangs. Also, giving sugary juices at bedtime can encourage cavities.

kicking

Sometimes called *quickening*, these flutter-like movements are the first perception by Mom of fetal movement. Quickening usually occurs around the twenty-week mark. At first, kicking is hardly noticeable, even to Mom. As time progresses, the kicking will get stronger and more intense, so that even dads can experience this exciting indication of Baby's presence. Sometimes Baby will kick Mom's sciatic nerve, which may shoot a severe pain down one or both of her legs. If you notice a sudden decrease in fetal movement, call your doctor.

kitchen safety (*see also* childproofing)

The kitchen can be a room of potential danger once Baby comes on the scene. Look under your kitchen sink. Do pesticides, strong cleaning solutions, or other liquids need to be moved to higher ground? Look in other low-lying drawers and cabinets. Do they contain sharp knives or mixing utensils with blades? Obviously you need to use caution around all the various parts of your house, but the kitchen needs extra attention. Always be careful with boiling hot water or when cooking with oil. Holding Baby in one arm while stirring with the other is not advised. And if anything hot is spilled on Baby's sensitive skin, the area should be closely examined. Begin now to look at the kitchen through your infant's eyes.

L

labeling

It's a good idea to label all the items in your diaper bag with your name. You may be taking the bag to a nursery, mother's-day-out program, or church facility. To avoid mix-ups with other infants' paraphernalia, put your baby's full name on all cups, bottles, pacifiers, and, of course, any medicine. When a nursery has fifteen to thirty babies in one room, it's easy to confuse diaper bags that basically all look the same. Label everything.

labor

The contracting of the uterus, which opens up the cervix to allow the actual delivery, is called *labor*. There's a good reason why it's called that. Labor is hard work. Many new, helpful medications are available today for the mother in labor. Yet even with all of today's current technologies, there's nothing quite like seeing your wife in that much pain. Many men report wanting to be of more help than they are able to offer. In other words, a feeling of helplessness sets in.

In most cases, labor is the culmination of nine months of waiting. Emotionally, physically, and mentally, everyone is on edge. There's a certain type of energy, a buzz, in the delivery room. Your baby is about to emerge on the scene, yet something could go wrong at the last minute, and everyone in the room knows it. All attention focuses on the delivery doctor, who knows more than anyone else in the room about the current condition of your baby. Your wife is probably sweaty and tired. Her muscles are sore; her energy drained. Delivery room nurses are getting black ink pads and weighing scales in order. It is precisely at this time that you need to be ready. Encourage your wife. Remind her that she's doing a tremendous job. Ask her if there's anything you can do to help. Can you cool her forehead, move a pillow, or feed her ice chips?

You'll never forget the first time you go through labor! Some moms are in such pain that they shout out words they'll later regret. Moms in intense labor have turned to their husbands and yelled, "This is your fault!" or "You're never touching me again!" or even "Why did you do this to me!" This type of thinking will pass—hopefully. We have also heard of men who have emerged from the delivery room with broken or fractured hands. How can a mom in labor break her husband's hand? If you're holding your wife's hand during one of the final pushes, watch out; you may end up holding your newborn with a cast up to your wrist.

Labor can be relatively quick—three or four hours—or long—up to twenty hours or more. If things fail to progress, your doctor may talk with you about performing a C-section.

Begin now to plan how you want to experience labor. Will you view this miracle through a video camera? Will you take still photos? Will you call the action play-by-play style over the phone to a loved one? Maybe you will take notes on a yellow legal pad. Whatever the case, make sure and be fully present for this amazing, once-in-a-lifetime event. You'll never again be a first-time father!

Lamaze classes (*see also* breathing)

Many organizations now offer pre-birth classes. You may not feel like attending these, but you should. You may feel silly carrying a set of pillows to these meetings, but you shouldn't. Take the lead and register you and your wife, and then be there. The normal routine at these classes consists of discussing your upcoming delivery with other couples, watching a film or two, and practicing breathing and relaxation techniques. Dad, when you attend and actively participate with your wife in these meetings, you are telling her that you also plan to be involved when d-day arrives. Some of the guys who snicker and scoff the most during the practice sessions are the very same ones who look like a deer caught in the headlights when the water breaks. Like a good Boy Scout, Dad, be prepared!

lotions

In the days and weeks leading up to the delivery, your wife's lower back can really hurt. Since there's so much weight being carried up front, the muscles in the back are being pulled and stretched in new ways. Find a lotion that's good for rubbing on your wife's aching back, swollen ankles, shoulders, and arms. She'll thank you for it.

···

When Things Don't Go as Planned
David A. Wheeler

What does one do when things don't go as planned? In most cases, everything we do in preparation for a child assumes that both Mother and Baby will be okay. The truth is, we don't like considering the alternatives, do we? Here's my story.

At approximately twenty-four weeks into my wife's second pregnancy, with no warning signs, her lungs began to bleed profusely. Within days, she was comatose in ICU, with the doctors warning that both she and the baby had a much greater chance of dying than living. "It will take a miracle," they said. Well, that's exactly what we got.

After nine long days of searching for answers, the doctors

finally diagnosed that she was suffering from a rare illness called Wegener Disease. The only medical remedy was large doses of chemotherapy—without knowing how the medication might affect the baby.

Quite frankly, the doctors feared the worst. "At this point, it doesn't appear that the baby is viable enough to survive the toxic chemicals," they said. Then they added, "There's a good chance the child may die this evening as we administer the first dose."

I bent over my wife's limp body and placed my hands on her stomach in order to feel the baby move. I didn't know if this would be the only communication I would ever have with this child. I only knew that I already loved her!

In the days following, much to the doctors' surprise, the baby appeared to be unaffected as her vital signs remained strong. Still, nothing could prepare us for what followed.

It was Saturday afternoon, December 2, 1989. I responded to an emergency call to respiratory ICU. When I arrived, it was obvious to me that something was seriously wrong as the doctors worked feverishly in my wife's room. I knew nothing of what was occurring; I simply prayed. It was then that the prenatal doctor wheeled out an incubator with my youngest daughter inside. She was fourteen inches long, weighing less than two pounds, with beautiful blue eyes, and only twenty-six weeks gestation. Believe it or not, she was literally birthed into a bedpan! We named her Kara, which means "God's most gracious gift."

Today, Kara is eleven years old and has mild cerebral palsy. Coping with her condition isn't easy for any of us, but she embraces life's challenges with great fervor and is truly God's angel of joy. She loves softball, church, friends, and fun! Like her mother, she is a beautiful young lady.

So . . . what does this communicate to prospective fathers?

First, trust God and be a man of prayer. After all, God is the giver of life. Second, keep your eyes on the journey, not the destination. That is, don't waste life; embrace it every day as a special gift. Finally, don't ever judge the gift by the size of the package.

Dr. David Wheeler serves as a professor at Liberty University in Lynchburg, Virginia.

M

mastitis

A breast infection, mastitis may or may not be accompanied by a fever and other flu-like symptoms. It can be caused by a breast milk duct that becomes plugged or infected. The breast can become very painful, engorged, red, hard, hot, or swollen. If any of these conditions persist, or if you notice pus or blood in the breast milk, contact your physician at once.

Moist heat applied prior to and during nursing can help milk to flow. Following feeding, you can assist your wife with ice applied to the affected areas and encourage her to rest in bed. She should also increase her fluid intake. Your doctor will most likely prescribe a two-week course of antibiotics.

maternity clothes

Colors, styles, fabrics, and fashions have all come a long way in the wonderful world of maternity clothes. Most of the moms we talk to, however, feel like "nothing fits" and "nothing looks good" during pregnancy. Since these clothes are only worn for a short period of time, many women borrow maternity clothes from friends and family. Dad, help your wife pick out nice outfits that she will feel good about. It's okay to wear an extra-large T-shirt around the house, but to help her feel special, find pretty maternity outfits (there are some out there), and make reservations for special evenings out.

maternity room (*see also* birthing room)

At some hospitals, the maternity room and the delivery room are two separate places. In these hospitals, you'll check into a maternity room; then as things start to progress, your wife will be wheeled into the delivery room, where your baby will actually be born. After a short time of cleanup, you will go back to your maternity room. Most hospitals now have LDR (labor, delivery, recovery) rooms. Moms labor, deliver, and recover all in the same room. Most of these rooms are decorated nicely with dim lighting and adequate furniture.

Many moms think they are not doing a good job of mothering unless they are with their baby the entire hospital stay. Actually, short periods away from Baby are a great time for her to catch an hour of sleep here and there. There will be plenty of time for interaction in the days to follow. If the hospital offers it, let the nurses monitor your baby for a few hours. They are trained to listen, observe, and intercept anything abnormal.

You don't want your wife coming home from the hospital exhausted. There may be times when you have to stand sentry at the door and tell folks that Mom is just too tired to accept any more visitors right now. Don't allow the maternity room to become Grand Central Station. You may also have to screen phone calls to limit the number of times your wife is asked to repeat the details of labor. All of these inquirers are well meaning, but Mom can become exhausted if you don't run interference.

moodiness

If your wife's hormones could be charted during pregnancy, they would follow the path of a bungee jumper. She may be going through periods of extreme moodiness. One minute she's laughing and the next, she's crying. Emotions are on edge. It's always best to talk through, at length, what she's feeling. Does she feel well prepared for the brand-new baby coming your way? Is she angry at how she looks or feels? Is she scared about the upcoming delivery? Is she mad at you for not helping more? This moodiness is normal. Tears may easily flow. Now is not the time to tease your wife about crying over a long-distance telephone advertisement. She may not even know exactly why she's feeling so sensitive or sad or mad.

morning sickness

The first few months of pregnancy can activate what has become known as morning sickness. Morning sickness does not mean there is something wrong with the baby. This malady will normally subside after the seventeenth week of pregnancy. Some moms report that drinking or eating certain foods like soda crackers, tea, fruit, or soft drinks brings relief. Like many other aspects of pregnancy, you will hear a myriad of home remedies or old wives' tales about how to overcome morning sickness. Here is ours: The trick is for your wife to eat soda crackers *before* she gets out of bed in the morning. Many new moms wait until mid-morning to eat some crackers, but it's too late at that point. In addition, some expectant moms get nauseous in the evening. No matter the time of day it sets in, folks still label it "morning sickness."

mother's day out

Churches, parishes, and other social institutions offer moms a break with various mother's-day-out programs. Dad, if you think it's easy taking care of a newborn day after day with no break in sight, try it for just one week. A good mother's-day-out program will allow your wife the chance to take a much needed breather. The sheer routine of providing care for a baby twenty-four hours a day can lead to mental and emotional exhaustion. Mom needs to go to a salon and have her hair and nails done. She needs to rest at home on a regular basis. In short, she needs relief! If she doesn't get away on a routine basis, she'll come apart. Enroll your baby in a quality mother's-day-out program. Trust us—Mom will thank you for it. If there is no such program in your area, see if there are trusted family members or friends who can provide some regular rotation of assistance.

movie theater

There are some places where Baby is simply not welcome. Some restaurants are off-limits. If your place of worship offers a nursery, utilize it. Babies' cries and biblical sermons don't mix well. And steer clear of taking your infant to a movie theater unless it is labeled as a "baby-friendly" showing. You may rationalize, "Our baby is sooooo quiet, and no one will care." Believe us, people *will* care. If your baby cries just a little bit, other movie goers will complain. And they have the right to. Some places just don't mix with infants. Over time you'll learn to distinguish which places are infant-friendly.

multiples

In 1995, a woman's chance of having twins was one in forty. About one-third of twins are identical, or monozygotic, twins (when one fertilized egg divides in half). Two-thirds are fraternal, or dizygotic, twins (when two eggs are fertilized by different sperm). It's a good idea to prepare for the possibility of a multiple birth. Most women who give birth to triplets or other multiples have undergone some type of fertility treatment—although one type, IUI (intrauterine insemination), where sperm are injected into a woman's uterus with a syringe, doesn't increase the risk of multiple fetuses.

Fertility drugs stimulate the ovaries, increasing the odds that several eggs will be released at the same time. On average, 25 percent of women taking a gonadotropin-releasing hormone (Pergonal) will become pregnant with at least twins. Chances are about the same if you have in vitro fertilization, because several eggs will be inserted into the womb to increase the chances of conception.

God will give you the grace to handle twins, triplets, or more. We believe He selects special couples who can handle this unique surprise. Do you remember the McCaughey family in Iowa who had septuplets—seven babies—in one delivery? We read about the fact that they scheduled a date night every Friday night. They probably needed it! And yet they made it work. A good suggestion is to talk with other parents who have experienced multiple births. It's also a good idea to join a club that celebrates multiple births with special activities and events.

music

Music is soothing. Many moms report that music helps them relax and focus during labor and delivery. Dad, try out some different musical styles and see what your wife likes best. It may be that she doesn't want any music at all. Yet she may find that hearing a familiar refrain brings continuity and comfort during this stressful time. In addition, stories are told about newborns becoming familiar with repetitive music. One expectant mom played the cello in her city's symphony. During her pregnancy, she was rehearsing a particularly difficult piece of music day after day for an upcoming performance. After the baby was born, the only music that would soothe this cranky baby was the exact same piece that had been heard over and over during the pregnancy.

N

naming

Picking out your baby's name can be tricky. Will you choose a long-standing family name? Will you go with a traditional yet unusual name? Will you use a different spelling of a common name? Will you select a name that could go with either a girl or boy, such as Chris or Kelly? Remember that your child will "wear" this name for many years to come. Try out the name for a while and see if it grows on either or both of you. The Lear family chose the pretty name of Crystal for their baby daughter, combining it with the middle name of Shanda. Try it out.

nap time

There are three keys to a smooth nap time: routine, routine, routine. Pick the same time and place for nap time. At the beginning stages, your baby will seem to nap all day long. That will quickly change. Then the routine will be two naps a day—the morning nap and the afternoon nap. Try to use the same routine for getting Baby down, including the same chair or room and even the same surroundings, like music or sounds. If Mom feels refreshed, nap time is a good opportunity to get something else accomplished. If Mom is as tired as Baby, however, she should be encouraged to lie down. Mom needs a nap as much as Baby, especially if she is breastfeeding at odd hours of the night. When your baby is little, you may want to put a sign on the front door that reads, "Knock quietly, Baby may be napping." There's nothing more frustrating than a door-to-door salesperson who wakes up a napping baby. You'll get upset, your baby will be tired, and the salesperson won't get a sale. Don't forget that as Baby grows and matures, naps become shorter in length and less frequent through the day.

nesting instinct

Dad, this one may be new for you. Have you heard of the nesting instinct yet? If you haven't, you'll see it in action soon. When Mom gets to about the eighth month, this natural, inborn instinct will kick in. Your wife will experience an extra burst of energy where she feels like cleaning the garage, the attic, the kitchen, the cars, the shed, the bedrooms, the laundry room, and the basement. What in the world is happening? Your wife is beginning to see her surroundings through different eyes. She sees dirt and germs in places she had never noticed before. She thinks, *I'm not taking my baby in there unless it's cleaned up.* So, Dad, roll up your sleeves and get ready to clean! The reason the nesting instinct kicks in now and not at the last minute is because your wife knows she'll be in no shape to do much work in the ninth month. At that final stage of pregnancy, she'll be doing well just to get around.

nipple confusion (*see also* bottle-feeding, breastfeeding)

If your baby is switched from bottle, to breast, to bottle, something called nipple confusion or nipple preference can set in. Problems arise when a breastfed baby is given an artificial nipple and then must try to learn to nurse from both breast and bottle. Why? Two different mouth and tongue motions and swallowing skills are required. In breastfeeding, the baby takes as much of the nipple and areola as possible into the mouth in order to pump the milk ducts.

The tongue is positioned beneath the nipple and is used to create a vacuum. In bottle-feeding, the baby uses the lips to grip the tip of the nipple. The tongue is placed in front of the nipple and is used to stop the flow of milk while swallowing.

Talk to your pediatrician about ways to reduce nipple confusion. Many different styles of bottle nipples can be found on the market. Always try to match them as closely as possible to each other or the real thing. If you are the only one at home and you sense this confusion setting in, don't worry, Dad. Come back again for the next feeding and your baby just might be hungry enough to forget about the differences and preferences in nipples.

nipples (*see also* breastfeeding)

If your wife is breastfeeding, her nipples can become sore, dry, even cracked. This condition is often caused when the baby doesn't take the nipple properly. The areola needs to be pulled into the baby's mouth, not the nipple only. The nipple should be farther back into the mouth, almost resting on the roof of the palate.

If sore nipples persist, your wife should avoid using soap on them and let them air dry. If the pain is severe, applying *pure* lanolin or vitamin E right from the capsule helps alleviate the soreness.

nursery

Another way you can assist during pregnancy is to help prepare the nursery. No matter where you are currently living, you can make some area of the house suitable for Baby. Pick a theme or color scheme you both like. Spend some evenings with your wife painting, papering, and decorating this special place. You can also use this time together to talk and dream about your new arrival.

Dad, when planning to prepare the nursery, keep in mind that Baby has his or her own schedule. He or she might arrive earlier than the doctor has predicted. Being prepared early for the baby to come home can help keep Mom's stress level down. It wasn't raining when

Noah began building the ark. In other words, don't start designing and constructing an elaborate nursery in the ninth month of the pregnancy.

nursing

See breastfeeding.

nurture

Many new dads feel uncomfortable about connecting with their baby on an emotional level. It doesn't feel "manly" to cuddle or coo with a baby. Yet it's important that new dads nurture their own babies. Nurturing is not the sole responsibility of the mother. Your baby needs the nurture of both you and Mom. Get involved from day one. We heard of one dad who was always sitting in the living room watching sporting events on television. After many weeks of this, Mom called out, "Honey, the baby needs changing. Do you think you could help out?" To this, the dad called out from behind the television, "Uh, yeah, honey, . . . I'll get the next one." After a few hours passed, the baby needed changing again. Remembering her husband's promise, Mom again called out, "Honey, the baby needs a diaper, and you said you would change the next one." Upon hearing this, the dad turned down the volume and announced, "When I said I would change the next one, I meant the next baby!" What a poor example of nurture! Dad, healthy fathers nurture their newborns in careful and loving ways. Be a hero and dive in from the start.

nutrition

Everything your wife eats while she's pregnant will eventually reach your baby. So it almost goes without saying that she needs to eat healthy foods—and Dad, you can help her do so. Many moms report sudden "cravings" during pregnancy. Don't dismiss this notion. It can be your baby's way of telling you he or she needs something specific. Some examples of healthy cravings include carrots, pickles, salad, and nuts. Mom needs to be careful, however, about eating too many sweets and unhealthy snacks. It's easy for your wife to think, "Well, I'm getting big anyway, I might as well eat all I want." Most of us know how difficult it is to lose weight. Many moms tell us it seems especially difficult to lose weight after having a baby. One insider tip: Forget the old adage of three square meals a day. Eating healthy snacks or very small meals every two to three hours usually works best for moms.

My Heart Exploded with Joy
Walt Kallestad

It all started with the flu. When the flu-like symptoms persisted, my wife, Mary, visited a doctor. The diagnosis wasn't what we expected at all—Mary and I were pregnant. Wow! It was good news that would change our lives for as long as we lived.

One of the first things we did was pray. We prayed for the pregnancy to go excellently. We prayed for the future of our unknown child. Also, we prayed that we might be the kind of parents God wanted us to be.

The following nine months were filled with preparing for our new arrival. We were excited—and scared. Having children was a dream that we shared. Nevertheless, we had never been parents before and didn't know what to do. So we read books, listened to tapes, and went to new-parent classes.

In the midst of everything else we were doing, Mary and I shopped for baby stuff and decorated a bedroom that would become our nursery. Finally, the day came when our firstborn, Patrick Gregory Kallestad, was born. His delivery ended up being very complicated. But after twenty-six hours of labor and a difficult delivery, our son arrived. When I first laid eyes on him, my heart exploded with joy. He was awesome!

Due to the use of delivery instruments, Patrick was noticeably bruised. Even so, with bruises and all, he was incredible. I counted carefully all ten fingers and all ten toes. As I continued to gawk in admiration at our beautiful "baldy" (when a baby is yours, bald is beautiful), tears of joy spilled down my cheeks. Through my tears, I prayed a big thank-you prayer. After all, Patrick was a miraculous gift from God.

I gave Patrick's mommy a great big kiss. Then I raced to the telephone and called everybody I could think of with the good news of the birth of our firstborn.

Words are inadequate to express the fantastic feelings of becoming a parent. Mary and I can truthfully tell you that now, even after thirty years of parenting, we are still as enthusiastic as the day we were told, "You are going to have a baby!"

My encouragement to every dad is,
- pray continuously,
- prepare vigorously,
- praise enthusiastically.

Dr. Kallestad serves as senior pastor of Community Church of Joy in Glendale, Arizona.

O

ob-gyn

Choosing an ob-gyn (doctor of obstetrics and gynecology) is an important, and sometimes difficult, personal task. Some couples prefer a woman. Some want a seasoned veteran who's delivered hundreds of babies. Others want a young doctor who, they reason, may be more up to date on the latest techniques. Some ob-gyns go to great lengths to make you, as a couple, feel relaxed and informed. Others share information on a need-to-know basis. Ask around when you select your ob-gyn. Here's a little hint: Make a visit to the hospital and ask delivery room nurses. They are up to speed on the styles and temperaments of the different doctors. If you live in a rural area, you may have limited options. No matter whom you choose, always feel free to ask that doctor your questions; no question is dumb. Don't suffer unnecessary stress worrying about a concern that your doctor could easily address.

object permanence

This is a strange phenomenon. Infants go through a time period when they think all objects they see are permanent. In other words, when your baby sees Mom, everything is okay. Then, a moment later, when Mom leaves the room, your baby may cry out loudly.

Why? Because Baby thinks Mom is gone for good! Hence the name: *object permanence.* This is why babies are so tickled by a simple game of peekaboo. If you smile at your baby, you'll get a big smile in return. But then, when you put a handkerchief over your face for a moment, your baby may get sad and even cry. Your baby thinks you are gone. Then, when you whisk the handkerchief away again . . . voila! You have magically reappeared! While object permanence can lead to fun, it can also lead to headaches. If you're at a restaurant, for instance, and you excuse yourself from the table, your baby may think you are leaving forever—and he or she will respond with obvious displeasure.

Oedipus complex

Simply described, the Oedipus complex is the emotional attachment of your toddler to the parent of the opposite sex. Dad, your little girl may begin to see you as her knight in shining armor or may even announce, "Daddy, I wish Mommy were gone so we could get married." Don't panic. This is a fairly common situation. Calmly help your son or daughter through this stage. Talk about the future, when your child will be married to someone his or her own age and how one day you may be grandparents to your son or daughter's own children. The short-term problem may manifest itself by your son's saying, "I hate you, Daddy!" or your daughter's getting mad at Mom for spending time with you. Sometimes, for example, when *we* hug or kiss at home, one of our younger children will run between us and try to separate us. Our boys push Paul away, and our girls push Pam away. This is the Oedipus complex at work.

opinion

Get ready for lots of unsolicited opinions. As soon as word gets out that you and your wife are expecting, advice will pour in on what you should be eating, wearing, and doing. If you're at a shopping mall and your wife is visibly showing, people you don't even know will approach your wife and pat her tummy. For whatever reason, people feel your excitement and want to offer help. If your baby has trouble of any kind, be ready for all sorts of homemade recipes, old wives' tales, and quirky advice. Some of this might even be helpful, but much of it can be dismissed. Just remember that everyone is entitled to his or her own opinion.

optimism

It takes a lot of optimism to be a good dad. You may at times look at your crying baby and wonder if he or she will ever mature. Have hope. And offer words of optimism to your wife. Tell her, "Someday this boy will be as tall as us," or, "I wonder what this girl is going to be good at when she grows up? Right now she can cry her lungs out; I wonder if she's going to be a singer." When you're feeling down and want to throw in the towel, allow yourself time to dream a little. Imagine what your little baby will look like five, ten, or twenty years from now. Without a clear and compelling vision of the future, it's easy to lose hope.

oral

Babies are oral creatures. They go through stages where everything they touch is put into their mouths. This includes dirt, rocks, toys, dog food, pet toys, coins, and paper clips. Be careful about leaving small things lying around. Your baby's fingers are not yet sensitive enough to feel what is being held. Thus, the object goes straight into the mouth. As you know, the mouth is highly sensitive, and the baby is feeling (and tasting) to see whether the object is sharp, rough, salty, or smooth. Rest assured, your baby should grow out of this oral stage. By the way, would you know what to do if your baby choked on a small object? Be sure to learn how to handle a choking situation by taking a local CPR class, and ask the instructor specifically about infants and toddlers.

organization (*see also* routine)

If you are not an organized person, your baby could move you in that direction. Babies are so small and yet they require so much stuff! You can't even walk out of the house without several bags and pieces of equipment. Follow the old rule of thumb that there's a place for everything, and everything should be kept in its place. Nothing is more frustrating than trying to get to a doctor's appointment on time when you can't find your baby's socks, shoes, and shot records. Get really organized about your bedtime routines. Go through a disciplined routine that alerts Baby, "It's time for sleep." An organized approach is also best for mealtimes. Sure, you can get creative at times, but most of the time, Baby prefers the comfort and security of a well-planned schedule.

Participative Parenting
Ted Budd

Other than the hormonal undulations, the endless appetite, and the monotonous sleeping positions, the first pregnancy is a time to be savored. You don't yet have to get a babysitter, and the only time the baby awakens both of you at night is when he or she drop kicks Mom's bladder.

I liken pregnancy to an engagement period. The woman does most of the work, but the man must look busy and interested. Picking out colors for the baby's room is like picking out the wedding napkins. When your wife shows you the decorating magazines, it doesn't matter what color you pick, only that you deliberate. I suggest that you hold your finger on the page of one example and flip intently between that one and another. Back and forth, back and forth, until you pick one color, but with only slight preference over the other. (That saves face in case she goes with the alternate.)

Pregnancy is a precursor to participative parenting. The length of gestation is a perfectly timed gift from God. Any shorter and the parents would go into shock. Any longer and she would go nuts. The nine months gave Amy Kate and me time to realize that our lives were really about to change, although we had no idea how. It gave us time to hold hands as we strolled in and out of baby stores. It gave me time to contemplate my new role, readjust my priorities, and realize that I'd have to exchange buying a Harley for a jogging stroller and a convertible for a minivan, and that I'd have to share Amy Kate's affection. It gave her time to nest, to make the cabinets safe for our ground-bound human, to nap, to snack, to read up on parenting styles and feeding methods, and pass on to me all that was relevant. Hint to new dads: care about all of the stuff! It's a presage of participative parenting.

When my oldest brother was born, my dad was at the YMCA, playing a vigorous game of pickup basketball. Times have changed. I was *there*. Amy Kate wanted me not just to be present but also to attentively participate. Our newborn was beautiful, not by his features—he was beet red, had a pointy noggin, and was slimy—but he was stamped with the image of God, and that made him beautiful. The labor and delivery was tiring, emotional, and gross at times, but I wouldn't have traded those moments for anything. Being there was the real beginning of participative parenting.

That was nearly a year ago. Our little guy isn't slimy, he isn't beet red, and his head is perfectly shaped, although still no hair. He's beautiful, and he makes me proud to be a father. I wonder where our portfolio of free time went, but I know it has been reinvested wisely in the raising of the next godly generation. I long to hear Amy Kate say to me in the evening, "You were a great dad today." I love meaningful compliments, and sometimes I ask her what made me so. She usually replies, "You were a participative parent."

Ted Budd is the owner of The T Paul Company LLC in Winston-Salem, North Carolina.

P

pabulum

This is an old-fashioned word for baby food. You may have a grand-parent ask, "Is the baby on pabulum yet?" or comment, "Well, of course she's crying all night. You're not giving her any pabulum." This early-stage food is normally a watery, easily absorbed rice- or oatmeal-based cereal.

pacifier

Here's an item that certainly hits a hot button. Should your baby calm himself or herself with a pacifier? What are the positives and negatives of choosing a pacifier over, say, rocking Baby until he or she calms down? Should you choose to employ a pacifier, strangers may approach you and say, "I can't believe you're letting that cute little guy suck on that ugly pacifier! We had seven babies and not one of them ever used that thing!" At that point, you may feel the urge to stick a pacifier in that person's mouth.

Infants have a strong natural, inborn desire to suckle. Some have a stronger need than others. A pacifier is simply one way to meet this need. It can calm down (pacify) your crying baby. It can also hold off your baby when he or she is hungry until your wife shows up or you can get to a bottle. The problem arises when you lose all fifty of your baby's pacifiers. Find a dad who has a squalling baby and no pacifier, and you can make a quick twenty bucks.

Some say a pacifier is better than allowing your infant to suck on his thumb because at the desired time you can remove the pacifier. (You'll want to keep the thumb.) Talk with your dentist about when to stop using pacifiers.

packing

Around two weeks before the due date, you should have your bags packed and ready to roll. Here's a list of some items to take to the hospital: lotion, camera (video and still), pajamas, snacks, money, phone numbers, reading material, toiletries, music, change of clothes, writing materials, laptop computer, and bottled water. Don't forget, you're packing not only for you and your wife but also for the baby, so you'll need a going-home outfit, socks, booties, and a blanket. You'll also need a safety-approved car seat for the baby to ride home in. The hospital will give you a take-home gift pack that contains some basic baby items, and you'll also be bringing home any gifts, cards, balloons, or flowers that others have dropped off or sent. The ride home can become quite a trip, so don't be shy about asking for help from friends. You can see that there will be lots of "stuff" to take home from the delivery room, so you may even need to plan on a couple of trips.

parenthood

You're entering into a new phase of your life. For at least the next eighteen years, you'll be parenting. You made it through your own adolescence, you made it to adulthood, and now you'll navigate parenthood. It's tough, no doubt about it. Some men go through periods of feeling trapped . . . of feeling like they want to hit the road and get away from it all. Parenthood takes all of your time, energy, and attention—that is, if you want to do a good job. But there is an end point. One day, you'll send off your youngest and you'll be an empty nester. Until then, remember this rule of thumb to guide you when the going gets tough and you feel like throwing in the towel: You're raising an adult, not a child. The goal is not to raise a toddler and keep him or her in toddlerhood. You're raising a future friend, so pour in your very best efforts.

patience

You may not be a patient man. And up until now you may have been able to hide that fact. That's getting ready to change. An infant can try your patience like nothing else. Are you the kind of guy who gets tired of waiting for traffic to move, long lines to budge, or paint to dry? We saw a guy yelling at a microwave oven the other day, "Hurry up!" Well . . . wait until you feed strained peas to a cranky toddler. Or hold your crying baby in a slow-moving line at the grocery store. Author Kevin Lehman calls the grocery checkout line *Armageddon.* (Get it? Arm-a-gettin'.) As your blood begins to boil, every grandmother within earshot will probably offer well-meaning advice: "Ahhh, poor baby. She wants her mama."

We've said this before, but we can't stress it enough: Don't ever shake your baby! Don't ever slap or spank an infant. It will do no good. If you feel like you've lost all patience or are angry at your baby, call a neighbor or a friend. Whatever you do, do not harm your baby. Parenting will make you more patient; and that's a good thing. So take a deep breath and realize that one day you'll thank your baby for making you a more patient man. (Besides, the little rascal just loves making the steam come out of your ears.)

pediatrician (*see also* well-baby checkups)

Pick a pediatrician with whom you'll be comfortable. Your pediatrician is a different doctor from your ob-gyn. Your pediatrician will normally make a first visit the day your baby is delivered just to make sure everything is okay. Then after returning home, you will bring your baby to the pediatrician's office for your baby's first official visit. Ask around to discover the different attributes of the pediatricians in your area.

pets

Sometimes pets and infants get along wonderfully. Sometimes they don't. Infants have been bitten, scratched, and even attacked by animals in the family. Pets are territorial, and since they've been in your home for a time they feel like the turf is theirs. Then you come home with a new little creature, and they feel like someone is invading their space. Get the picture? Go slow with mixing Baby and any pet. Certain dogs, such as German shepherds, pit bulls, and Dalmatians, can harm babies by being too rough. Cats can curl up with Baby in the crib, creating the risk of suffocation. Always exercise caution around animals. It is thought that the reason ferrets scratch, claw, or bite at a baby's mouth is because of the milk scent. When animals are around babies, even the calmest of pets can do the unexpected.

Some babies are allergic to certain animals. Be willing to part with a pet, if necessary, for your baby's health.

Pregnant moms should not regularly clean a cat's litter box because of the risk of contracting toxoplasmosis, an infection that can result in miscarriage, stillbirth, or birth defects.

phone calls

Even though most cell phones can be turned off or set to vibrate, there are few things as frustrating for you as your tired baby being wakened by a telephone solicitor or a random phone call. You may also begin to tell friends and family members to please call before 9:00 or 10:00 PM. Your old high school and college buddies who have yet to discover the joys of fatherhood probably won't understand. But your wife and baby will thank you for putting a stop to the 1:00 AM call that awakens your sleeping baby and begins, "Hey, dude, did you just see the ending of the Lakers game?"

photos

What type of photos, if any, do you want taken during the delivery? Modesty requires you keep the "last-minute-baby-is-coming-out" pictures in a private place for only close family members. Guests in your home don't normally prefer to see the action shots, but instead love to see your newborn after he or she has been cleaned up and wrapped in a blanket. Also, almost all hospitals offer a photo service where your baby will be photographed on the day you plan to leave. So pack a nice infant outfit for this first official portrait. If you have the technological capabilities, you can also send your newborn's photos through your computer or phone to friends and family members in other cities and states. Discuss the subject of photos with your wife before you start clicking away.

placenta

The placenta is a pancake-shaped organ that develops in the uterus just twelve days after conception. It provides the nutrients for your baby and eliminates his or her waste products. It is commonly referred to as the afterbirth because it's delivered after the baby.

placenta previa

This is a pregnancy-related condition in which the placenta is attached too low on the uterine wall, fully or partially covering the opening of the uterus. The condition can cause hemorrhaging in late pregnancy or can make vaginal delivery prohibitive.

planning the route

Are you ready to play race car driver? All new dads secretly fantasize about streaking through town with their screaming, expectant wife and a blazing police escort. Doesn't usually happen. It's not a good idea to speed through town anyway. What could be worse than getting into an accident on your way to the hospital? At worst, one of you could get hurt, and even a minor fender bender would delay you.

You should be prepared, however, to make it to the delivery room in the shortest time possible. You can employ little time savers. Do you know, for example, which hospital entrance to use? Do you know where to park? Where to check in once you arrive? Will you have your suitcase packed and the car vacuumed?

playground

When you take your baby to a public playground, be ready for the usual comments. Even if you provide care on a regular basis, moms may welcome you with, "Oh, Dad has the baby today, huh?" or "It must be Mommy's day off today." Always be careful on playgrounds. Older children can get carried away and run over your toddler. Also, if the park is a public area with lots of kids, you'll need to keep a keen eye on your baby. We have actually seen a new dad reading a sports magazine while his youngster wandered off. Not a good idea!

Be cautious concerning the equipment as well. Is any exposed metal extra hot from the sun? Is rusty metal waiting to cut your baby's sensitive skin? Are the swings in good working order? Be careful to put your baby in the right-size swing. Small babies do not have the grip yet to hold onto chain swings; they need the "bucket swings" they can sit down in. The rule of thumb is to follow your baby around the playground pretty closely while he or she is small. More freedom comes as your toddler grows.

play group

Many new parents implement a play group—a group of friends who have children of similar ages and who gather together on a regular basis. These groups can move from home to home or from one activity to another. Some require the mom or dad to be present; others allow you to simply drop off your child. A play group is a good place for your child to learn some basic rules about sharing. Ground rules should be set between the parents too; otherwise, subtle verbal sparring matches can break out. "I saw your boy hit my girl!" "Oh, my little boy would never do that. I think your girl just fell down." You get the picture.

playmates

It's a good idea to introduce some playmates to your toddler at an early age. Remember, your baby feels the entire world centers around him or her. (And in many ways it does!) A playmate will help your child learn there are others in the world besides Mommy and Daddy. But realize that your baby doesn't know how to share. So don't be shocked when he pulls a toy away from his first playmate. This is normal. It's also normal for your baby to hit, push, or bite other playmates; this behavior cannot, however, be tolerated. Appropriate discipline will teach your toddler the rules of human interaction. It's likely you'll run into other parents who feel their babies were born with no sin nature. They may even exclaim, "Oh no, that wasn't Johnny! He would never push another child. I'm sure your baby just tripped." So playmate time can become as much a learning experience for some parents as it can for toddlers. Just be prepared when perfect little Johnny smacks your child in plain sight of everyone—everyone, that is, except Johnny's mom. Prepare to exercise and receive grace with the other parents in your play group.

post-mature

Any infant born at forty-two weeks gestation or later is considered post-mature. As when a baby is premature, his or her being post-mature can lead to complications. The baby may be larger and less able to pass through the birth canal, or the placenta may no longer be able to provide adequate oxygen or nutrition. Most doctors will call in an expectant mom at forty weeks to begin a close monitoring of her condition. Nonetheless, call your doctor if your wife is at the forty-two week stage. Babies have a mind of their own. Some come early, some late.

postpartum depression (*see also* blues)

In the days and weeks after delivery, your wife may go through a period of slight or severe depression. Some moms call it the "baby blues," but if it lasts more than a couple of weeks, it could be postpartum depression and she should see her doctor. You can see how mild depression might develop. For nine months, excitement has been building over the upcoming delivery. Then in one day—normally—it's all over. Along with the big hormonal shift that occurs after delivery, the hard work sets in. There's loads of laundry, mountains of messes, spilled bottles, dirty diapers, and the visitors have all gone home. This is not the time to tell your wife to "buck up!" It's actually your time to pitch in and help out even more. Why not take a week off from work and play Mr. Mom for a spell. (Some of you may be doing that already, we know!) Let Mom get out of the house for a while to regain her excitement about being a mother. Bring home a gift or have one of your wife's friends come and spend a couple of days to help out. Follow your doctor's advice, and do whatever it takes to get your wife through this postpartum period. This is a very serious condition and should not be taken lightly.

potty training

Here is a monster subject. Entire volumes have been written on this topic, and it's a good idea to read at least one. Toilet training can be boiled down to this: it is the process of teaching your toddler how to control his or her urination and bowel movements. There are many different approaches. Our advice is not to force or pressure your toddler into being fully toilet trained by a certain age. Putting pressure on your child only increases his or her anxiety. On the other hand, you can actually make the process fun. For our boys, we place Cheerios in the toilet bowl and have them "aim" at them. They love it! Or you may want to purchase a small potty-chair so your toddler can sit next to you. Focusing on your son or daughter staying dry is one of the keys. Tell your child, "Mommy and Daddy are so proud of you now that you know how to stay dry! It sure feels good to stay dry, doesn't it?" Focusing on the positive is far better than saying, "You're wet again. I'm so disappointed in you! You're always wet!" Lots of people will provide advice to you on this touchy subject. But remember, each toddler is unique and will develop at their unique pace.

powder

Using baby powder, talcum powder, or cornstarch on your baby's bottom to prevent diaper rash is no longer recommended. Traditional talc creates airborne powder that can cause respiratory distress, and cornstarch becomes an abrasive when it gets wet. There are now safe alternatives, such as Patty Cake Dustless Baby Powder, a talc- and cornstarch-free pressed compact that is applied with a disposable cotton applicator.

prayer

Pray for your wife and your baby on a regular basis. Pray that God will teach you how to be a loving dad. Pray for protection, joy, and insight throughout the nine months of the pregnancy. Pray, pray, pray! God promises to hear and answer your prayers. Ask others to pray for you. When people ask how they can help, ask them to pray, and then give them something specific to pray for. You may want to write down some of these prayers so you can show your son or daughter how you were depending on God in faith to provide for all of your needs during your child's days of early development.

premature

This term is used to describe any baby born before thirty-seven weeks of gestation. Fewer than ten percent of babies arrive this early. If your baby is born prematurely, he or she will be required to stay in the hospital until healthy enough to go home. Most neonatal intensive care units allow long visiting hours for parents and grandparents but don't allow for other visitors. The nurses and doctors work very hard to provide the best possible care for your baby. It can be a stress-filled environment, but know that they are trying their best to get your baby home to you.

prolapsed cord

In one of every three hundred or so births, the umbilical cord slips out through the cervix ahead of the baby. This is dangerous because uterine contractions block blood flow to the baby. Unless the cervix is already dilated and birth is imminent, cesarean delivery is the usual solution.

protection

One of the traits of the involved father is a strong desire to protect his wife and baby. In today's violent world, there are those who wish to harm the ones you love most. Rapists and pedophiles are on the lookout for unprotected, unguarded families. Become a protective father! Go the extra distance in watching and looking out for your new family. You may have become accustomed to your wife's driving to the store late at night. Now, however, she may be carrying your new baby in one arm and trying to load groceries or packages with the other. It's normal and healthy to allow others to watch your child while you and your wife take some time alone together. But in today's sad society, it is essential to do background checks on nursery workers, babysitters, and caregivers. You are the God-ordained protector of your family. Be a good one.

. . . .

Hear, My Son
Paul Pettit

Of all the jobs I've ever held, this one is the hardest. I've planted strawberries in the summer and Christmas trees in the fall, but my current job takes more faith. I've delivered radio newscasts to nationwide audiences, but I need even more coolness and calmness for my present assignment. One year I served as laundryman for the entire University of Kansas football team, but this current job can be even more humbling. Unless you've experienced it firsthand, you'll probably laugh like I used to and ask, "How hard can it be?" In case you haven't guessed, I'm writing about fathering.

I want my kids to grow up healthy, so I try to give them a fairly balanced diet. I want my children to have manners, so I teach them "please" and "thank you" and "may I?" I want my kids to be emotionally stable, so I help them laugh at their mistakes. But there's one character trait, one value, I want them to possess more than any other. I want my children to become wise.

The common definition of wisdom is "skill for living." It takes wisdom to walk life's journey, wouldn't you agree? How many times have you wished you could take back a purchase you really shouldn't have made? Have you ever said yes to an oily salesman and later spent an evening realizing you failed to make a wise decision?

Lots of folks are smart. You can get smart by reading books. But not all smart people are wise. True, wisdom includes knowledge, but wisdom is more than intelligence . . . much more. Wisdom is worth dying for. Yet where does one go for wisdom? If it is indeed crying out from the streets, as the Bible says, how come so few people ever bump into it?

Poor behavior patterns are passed down from generation to generation. You are blessed if your parents took more than a passing interest in you. And you are fortunate indeed if your mother or father pointed out ways to live wisely. Parents can give their sons and daughters tips on making it to the finish line of life. Books too can provide advice for avoiding pitfalls. Short stories and fables contain morals and maxims that help open our eyes to the dangers around us. For the handbook of handbooks, however, look no further than the Bible. The Word of God is a veritable mother lode of wisdom literature. The Good Book tells us, in fact, that wisdom itself comes from the Author.

First, though, let's make sure we're talking about the right kind of wisdom. The New Testament writer James reminds us that there are two distinct kinds.

> Who is wise and understanding among you? Let him show it by his good life, by deeds done in the humility that comes from wisdom. But if you harbor bitter envy and selfish ambition in your hearts, do not boast about it or deny the truth. Such "wisdom" does not come down from heaven but is earthly, unspiritual, of the devil. For where you have envy and selfish ambition, there you find disorder and every evil practice. But the wisdom that comes from heaven is first of all pure; then peace-loving, considerate, submissive, full of mercy and good fruit, impartial and sincere. (James 3:13–17)

Make sure you seek the "coming down from heaven" kind of wisdom. That's the kind your children will use their entire lives.

Remember what we keep saying: You're not raising children, you're raising adults. And children need wisdom to navigate through to adulthood. Who among us would give the car keys to our eight-year-old with the instructions, "Hang in there 'til you get it right. Driving is hard, and you'll probably get some bangs and bruises, but keep on driving!" Of course that would be foolish. Neither should we expect our sons and daughters to figure out wise living on their own.

Our bookstores are filled with advice on raising kids. But you can do no better than the "big five": Job, Psalms, Proverbs, Ecclesiastes, and Song of Solomon. Many scholars refer to them collectively as the Wisdom Literature of the Bible. Focusing on God's ways and means for correct living, this section literally overflows with advice and admonition. You could pay a consultant millions and receive no better advice than this treasure trove.

Especially helpful is Proverbs 1–9. In this section, two things are happening in abundance: teaching and learning. The teaching is carried out by a father, and the learning is undertaken by a son. It is assumed that what the father possesses, the son is lacking. What is never assumed, however, is that what the father has, the son desires. In fact, left to his own devices or ignoring the instruction of his dad, the son becomes what every parent fears: a fool. The fool is pictured as a bumbling dunce, a senseless creature no smarter than an ox that heads blindly into a ditch. The wise son looks, listens, and learns from his devoted dad. The dad teaches the boy how to handle girls (especially the flirtatious kind), money (how to keep it and how to spend it), nature (how to observe and learn from it), and life itself (how to live it to the fullest).

Recently I have been teaching my own kids about consequences. I broke down the word for them, since they admitted they didn't know what it meant, and told them it meant "a pattern."

"The word *sequence*," I said, "means 'one thing after another.' When you put the word *con* in front, which means 'with,' you have 'one thing which affects another.'"

They seemed duly impressed but went right on licking their ice-cream cones. "Lauren," I said, "give me a pattern of events that affect each other."

"Uhmmm . . . I dunno," she muttered.

"Well," I prodded, "when you eat too much ice cream you gain weight. Or when you stay up too late at night, how do you feel in the morning?"

"Grouchy," she said.

"Right! You got it!" Then I turned to one of my sons. "Evan," I said, "give me another consequence."

"Like . . . um . . . when I get out of my car seat, the policeman will stop us," he said, repeating an often-heard warning in our minivan.

"Or if you drive too fast, you'll get a ticket," my wife added, smiling.

The cry of Proverbs 1–9 is "Hear, my son!" And it should be a lesson to parents as well. More than likely, you put in a full day at work. Like me, when you get home, you want to put up your feet and relax. But another full-time job is waiting when you pull into the driveway. As your "learners" fly out the front door and race down the driveway, your role as their teacher begins. The classroom is wherever you decide it should be. The lessons are waiting all around you. So go on, dole out some wisdom today! Your kids will thank you for it later.

Parenting is a tough job. There seem to be few immediate rewards. Sure, our kids bring to us their take-home Sunday school lessons and vacation Bible school art, but it gets piled together with last month's bills and yesterday's birthday cards. So, like the farmer who patiently cares for his crops, the wise parent takes the long view when investing in his sons and daughters. Wisdom's dividends pay nicely. Keep at it. Don't get discouraged. What you are now dealing with is not the final product. The investor who constantly buys and sells, fidgeting with his stock portfolio, seldom makes money over the long haul. Parenting takes a steady hand and a watchful eye. Many of the silly little annoyances will pass, but cracks in character must be dealt with swiftly. Remember the rewards. Having your child acquire wisdom is well worth the struggle. For "blessed is the man who finds wisdom, the man who gains understanding, for she is more profitable than silver and yields better returns than gold" (Prov. 3:13–14).

queasiness (*see also* blood)

There's nothing wrong with feeling a little queasy about the delivery. Many men feel faint seeing their own wife in such a distressing condition. There's nothing unmanly about requesting a few minutes to lie down or to take a brisk walk outside to cool off. It's better to be prepared for the hours after delivery than to pass out or be admitted for falling and hitting your head on a table. Be prepared to see lots of blood and tissue during labor; bringing another life into this world is not without blood, sweat, and tears. If you become faint at the sight of blood, plan to stand by your wife's side and look into her eyes. Wait to look at your new baby until the doctor hands him or her up to lie on your wife's chest. There's no reason to push the envelope if you easily become queasy. You can feel free to politely pass if the doctor asks you to move down to the foot of the bed to assist.

questions

Most dads have tons of questions about babies, labor, and delivery but are nervous about asking. For a variety of reasons, moms normally don't share this same fear. Women gather in groups frequently to discuss all types of subjects related to babies. But can you imagine sitting around with a bunch of guys and asking, "Hey, Ted, do you think my boy's circumcision is healing properly?" We urge you to cast aside any fears about asking questions and ask away. Ask lots of questions; the more, the merrier. There is absolutely no dumb question when it comes to pregnancy and childbearing. Ask other dads, ask other moms, ask grandparents, ask doctors and nurses. The well-informed dad makes the best dad. We have seen dads who stand by quietly while a mom asks, "He wants to know if . . . ?" The day of dad waiting outside of the delivery room is over. Put on your hospital scrubs, wash up, and ask questions!

quitting

Mark our words: there will come a day, Dad, when you feel like throwing in the towel. After a few particularly difficult nights or days with your newborn, you may experience a strange sensation of wanting to leave your responsibilities behind. This is normal. Fathers through the ages have felt like jumping in the chariot and getting out of Rome. But think about it. In the long run, how will this really help? What good will it do to abandon your wife and baby? God has given you the responsibility of caring for your family. He feels you can handle it. Don't quit on your family. Trust God.

There are many ways to quit on your family. Some dads actually leave town. Others begin spending evenings at work or in leisure activities. Others take drugs or start drinking heavily. We're not denying being a dad is a heavy responsibility—probably the toughest task you'll ever take on, if you're serious about being a good father. But quitting won't help. It'll only cause more problems, pain, and confusion. Ask God the Father to give you the strength to carry on. When you're an old man surrounded by grandchildren and great-grandchildren, you'll be glad you stayed the fathering course.

R

rash (*see also* diaper rash)

Your baby will probably get lots of rashes. Any reddish spot or patch of irritated skin can be considered a rash. Rashes can be caused by illnesses, allergies, or heat, and are usually temporary. Don't allow rashes to go unattended. After a few days, if the rash doesn't go away, see your doctor.

reading to Baby

Dad, it's never too early to read to your baby. Your tiny infant is able to recognize the difference between your voice and your wife's voice. Turn off the television and read or just talk to your baby.

recalls

Pay attention to recalls on baby products that you buy. From baby strollers that present a risk to parents to pacifiers that present a choking hazard to Baby, every year scores of products are found to pose an unexpected safety risk to consumers. The best way to ensure that you learn about recalls on your major purchases is to register them.

reflux

See colic, spit-up.

rooting reflex

This is one of the reflexes present at birth. Your baby will automatically turn his head and start sucking when his cheeks are stroked. Some think their baby is saying, "No . . . no . . . no, I don't want any more." But your baby is not saying no, he's only expressing the rooting reflex.

routine (*see also* organization)

Get into a routine from day one. Try to set up a schedule that works well for both you and your wife. Dad, this is where you need to be highly involved. When your wife first returns from the hospital, she'll be very tired. Now is your time to help with feeding and changing on a routine basis. In addition to taking over duties around the home, maybe you'll volunteer to do the 2:00 or 3:00 AM feeding. No, we're not kidding. Other routines should set in as well, such as changing, bathing, stroller rides, and naps. Babies need the security that schedules provide. In addition, many new dads now take paternity leave from work.

rubella

This is a mild, highly contagious viral disease (known more commonly as the German measles) that can cause serious birth defects if your wife is afflicted. Women who haven't had the disease should be immunized before conception.

· ·

A Great Dad
James Dobson

Someone has said, "Link a boy to the right man, and he will seldom go wrong." That adage is even more accurate when the "right man" happens to be his dad.

The influence of a good father is incalculable. I was blessed to have had that kind of dad. He was a wonderful man—not because of his accomplishments or successes. He was great because of the way he lived his life, his devotion to Jesus Christ, and the love he expressed for his family.

Some of my favorite memories are the times we spent together. We'd get up very early on a wintry morning, put on our hunting clothes, and head twenty miles out of town to our favorite place. We'd climb over the fence and follow a little creek for several miles leading to an area that I called "the big woods," because the trees looked so huge to me. Dad would get me situated under a fallen tree that made a secret room, and then we'd wait for the sun to rise. The entire panorama of nature would unfold out there in the woods as the squirrels, chipmunks, and birds awakened before us.

Those moments together with my dad were priceless to me. Conversations occurred out there that didn't happen anywhere else. How could I have gotten angry at a dad who took the time to be with me? The interactions we shared in that setting made me want to be like that man—to adopt his values as my values, his dreams as my dreams, and his God as my God. His pervasive influence continues in my life today. That's the power of a man to set a kid on the right road.

Taken from Dr. Dobson's Focus on the Family Bulletin, *June 2000. Published by Tyndale House, Wheaton, Illinois. Used by permission.*

Dr. James Dobson, who lives in Colorado Springs, Colorado, is the author of numerous best-selling books and is heard daily on the radio broadcast Family Talk.

S

scarlet fever

This condition is named for the bright red rash it produces. Scarlet fever is caused by the same bacteria responsible for strep throat and is most common in children between ages two and ten. Scarlet fever is treated with antibiotics.

security

Your baby has spent nine months in the safe and secure world of his or her mother's womb. Now your baby is thrust into a cold, sometimes uncaring, world. He or she needs security. Babies like to be wrapped snugly in a blanket or held firmly in your arms. If your baby is held loosely or is lying on his or her back—for a diaper change or bath, for instance—he or she will feel insecure and threatened. You get the picture. Help your baby feel secure. A secure baby is a happy baby.

separation anxiety (*see also* object permanence)

When an infant or toddler is anxious about being away from his or her primary caregiver, the crying or screaming will begin. Infants can experience separation anxiety as early as seven months, but it usually peaks between a year and eighteen months. Some babies will not experience this condition much at all, while others will scream if Mom or Dad simply leaves the room.

sex

See intercourse.

shaken baby syndrome

Severe injuries can result when a baby (or child) is shaken. Common results include swelling of the brain, hemorrhaging, and neck injuries. In extreme cases, shaken baby syndrome is fatal. No matter how frustrated you become, never, *never*, shake your baby. It will bring nothing but harm.

shoes

Your baby does not need shoes for proper foot development. But shoes are good for protection when your baby is learning to walk. In cold weather, you will want to have your baby wear gloves and booties for protection from the elements. You may not think the temperature is very cold; however, a newborn has sensitive skin, so in wintertime or very cold weather, little fingers and toes need to be bundled up.

SIDS

Hearing about Sudden Infant Death Syndrome (SIDS) strikes fear into the heart of every new dad. A primary goal of any dad is to protect his new baby. But this traumatic disorder can happen in the middle of the night and for no apparent reason. SIDS usually strikes infants between the ages of one month and twelve months. These are the times when you will have to totally trust in the Lord. From the very start, you have to put your baby in the Lord's arms. Your baby is His, on loan to you from God. You are a steward. So learn all you can about reducing the risk of SIDS. But at some point, you'll have to go to sleep yourself and leave your baby in your Father's care.

To reduce the risk of SIDS, pediatricians now recommend putting your babies to sleep on their backs or sides. They also recommend a firm, tight-fitting mattress for the crib, with all comforters, pillows, and stuffed animals removed. Pregnant women should stay away from cigarettes, and smoking should not be allowed in your home after Baby is born. Also, make sure that your baby is not over-bundled, even in the cold of winter.

sitz bath

The day after delivery, nurses will probably have your wife take a sitz bath. The shallow, tepid water moves around in the tub while Mom remains still. Sitz baths are recommended to soothe the discomfort and pain of hemorrhoids or episiotomy stitches.

sleeping (*see also* SIDS)

Getting your baby to "sleep like a baby" isn't always easy. Entire libraries have been written on how to get babies to sleep through the night. It's helpful to establish a regular routine for getting your baby to sleep and to put him or her to bed at the same time each evening. The *Journal of Pediatric Medicine* recommends placing your baby on his or her back or side to reduce the risk of SIDS.

God has given moms a very strong instinct to know when an infant needs breastfeeding or simply the comfort of being held. Learn to differentiate between the subtleties of your baby's various cries. The ultimate goal is for all three of you to get some rest. If that involves one of you getting up to comfort Baby for a short time, we feel it's worth it. However, remember that sleep habits are very difficult to break once they are established. If you begin a sleeping routine that works well, it will be difficult to change. For example, if you allow Baby to sleep in your bed, that pattern will become a routine that is quite difficult to break once you feel it is time to move Baby out.

spanking

To spank or not to spank is another hot-button issue with parents. However you decide, you and your wife need to agree on how you are going to discipline your child. Spend time talking and praying through the subject of discipline. Discuss the ways your own parents disciplined you.

An infant is not able to willfully disobey. Spanking or shaking your infant only does harm.

Between seventeen and twenty-four months of age, you'll know that your toddler is willfully disobeying, and you may decide to provide a firm swat on the fatty area of the buttocks. Never slap or hit your toddler. Many parents use a wooden spoon or paddle to differentiate between the hand that loves and the paddle that represents the parents' authority—and you do need to be the authority. Your toddler is constantly on the lookout for boundaries. Provide them in a loving yet firm manner. Your toddler needs to know that a hot stove will burn their hand, not all dogs are friendly, and the street is a place designated for automobiles.

spit-up

It's normal for your baby to spit up after feedings. But if your baby spits up quite a bit after every feeding, he or she may have reflux. This is a condition where food is not being digested properly. It can cause weight loss, and there is a burning sensation as the acidic foods are brought back up through the esophagus.

After feedings, be prepared with a baby towel. Pettit's law for spit-up is as follows: Your baby's chances of spitting up all over you are in direct proportion to the cost of your suit and the importance of the meeting to which you are headed.

stool (*see also* diarrhea)

A baby can go several days without making stool. The key is to watch for changes in stool. Introducing different foods can produce an array of changes. Some of these foods may cause an allergy that can show up as diarrhea. If you notice a consistent pattern of changes in stools, your baby may not be feeling well, and you should consult your doctor.

The first few diapers will contain a small amount of stool, and it is normal for the stool to be very dark in color. After breast milk or formula is introduced, the stool will change and become yellow. Then when solids are introduced, the color and consistency will remain constant, brown, and firmly compact.

strangulation

See suffocation.

stress

Providing care for a baby over a long period of time can produce high levels of stress, so parenting breaks are a necessity. When you are experiencing a lot of stress, your parenting skills are vastly diminished. Discover what activities reduce your stress and get involved on a regular basis. Dads, this means giving your wife a regular break if she is the one providing the majority of care. We're serious. Some dads give lip service but not real parenting service when it comes to relieving Mom on the front lines. Dad, be a hero at home and jump into the fray! We strongly recommend fully co-parenting and sharing all household chores.

stretch marks

Hey guys, imagine walking around all day with a twenty-pound bowling ball in your abdomen. Can you imagine what that would do to your muscles and skin? In the ninth month of pregnancy, your wife's skin has stretched to the breaking point. Then the baby is delivered, and the skin quickly recovers. Yet stretch marks remain. The elasticity of the skin is really a miracle of God. Moms, however, don't see stretch marks as a miracle. They become the bane of swimming suit season. There is no quick cure. Over time, however, stretch marks may diminish in appearance. Making fun of your wife's stretch marks is a *baaaaaaaaad* idea! A smart comment will sentence you to one free night on the back porch.

stroller (*see also* recalls)

Spend some time shopping for a quality stroller. Hundreds of designs are now on the market, but strollers come in two basic types. One is the lightweight model that can be taken out on the spur of the moment for a quick walk down the sidewalk. The other is the heavy-duty, all-day shopping variety that can hold enough equipment to climb Mount Everest. If you are going on an all-day outing, you will want a stroller that can hold diapers, toys, and snacks. It's a good idea, too, to get a stroller with a sun shield. All strollers get filthy after a few months. It's simply the result of constantly moving your peanut-butter-and-jelly-covered child in and out of his or her ride all day. We like to take our strollers out to the driveway and hose them down and scrub them with soap and a brush once in a while to get them looking good as new. Inspect your stroller on a regular basis to ensure it is not pinching or cutting your child's soft skin.

suffocation

When you place your infant in the crib, don't put stuffed animals or toys all around the head. Let the infant sleep in an empty crib during the first few months. Also be careful with your baby around balloons or plastic bags. It's easy for Baby to accidentally get plastic stuck around his face, mouth, or nose. A baby can suffocate in three to four minutes. Do you know CPR? Now that you're a father, you need to learn the proper technique.

Make certain to childproof your house. A baby can strangle on an electrical cord or suffocate on a plastic bag. Read through some of the safety literature your pediatrician can provide. Carefully check baby clothing for drawstrings or hats that tie under the chin. Crib toys, decorations, bedding, blinds, and curtains should have no cords or pull strings that could entangle an infant.

sunburn

An infant's skin is highly sensitive. Apply extra-protective sunscreen lotion on Baby if you are going to be out in the sun for an extended period of time. White zinc oxide is a good sunscreen to spread on faces, shoulders, and arms. Teach your child to wear a hat at a young age. Prolonged exposure to the sun can also be harmful to Baby's eyes, so try to keep them shaded. Dermatologists now report that one of the predictors of adult skin cancer is the cumulative amount of sun exposure a person has had throughout life. In other words, the skin seems to "save up" repeated sunburns.

swimming pools

Never leave an infant or child unattended around a swimming pool, lake, stream, or river. Never. If you are leaving a toddler or young child in the care of another person, inquire about swimming pools or other bodies of water nearby. Is the pool fully enclosed? Does it have self-latching gates? Will other children be using the pool area? Again, never take a chance when it comes to water safety. If you do enjoy water activities, be sure your child is equipped with a Coast Guard–approved personal flotation device designed specifically for children. Don't use an adult device for a child. Enroll your toddler in a water acclimation class or beginners swim class as soon as they are old enough.

swings

See playground.

··

"I Want to Be Just Like You"
Lyrics by: Dan Dean and Joy Becker

The lyrics to this popular song capture the feel of a father's heart:
He climbs in my lap for a goodnight hug;

He calls me Dad and I call him Bub.
With his faded old pillow and a bear named Pooh
He snuggles up close and says, "I want to be like you."
I tuck him in bed and kiss him goodnight;
Trippin' over the toys as I turn out the light.
And I whisper a prayer that someday he'll see
He's got a father in God 'cause he's seen Jesus in me.
Lord I want to be just like You
'Cause he wants to be just like me.
I want to be a holy example
For his innocent eyes to see.
Help me be a living Bible, Lord,
That my little boy can read.
I want to be just like You
'Cause he wants to be like me.

Got to admit I've got so far to go.
Make so many mistakes and I'm sure that you know
Sometimes it seems no matter how hard I try
With all the pressures in life I just can't get it all right.
But I'm trying so hard to learn from the best
Being patient and kind, filled with Your tenderness.
'Cause I know that he'll learn from the things that he sees
And the Jesus he finds will be the Jesus in me.
Right now from where he stands I may seem mighty tall
But it's only 'cause I'm learning from the best Father of
them all.

T

talking with Baby

Dad, start talking to your baby from the very start. We know, we know . . . it doesn't feel masculine to talk to a baby in the womb. You'll feel like you are talking to your wife's tummy. Do it anyway. While still in the womb, your baby can tell the difference between sounds, including voices. Besides, talking to your baby in the womb does wonders for your relationship with your wife. It tells her that you're interested and concerned. It shows that you're going to be an involved and helpful parent. So pull up a chair and start talking. Come on, you can spit it out! Work on getting over this emotional hurdle. Break through the intimacy barriers and whisper to your baby, "Hey, this is your daddy here. I can't wait to see you. Your mom and I are getting your room ready. I love you, and I'll be here for you." We believe someone should produce a bumper sticker that reads, *Real men talk to their babies in the womb!*

teething

Here come the teeth . . . here come the teeth. How do you know? Indicators can include diarrhea, crying, constant drooling, and biting. Run your forefinger along your baby's gums. If they look or feel swollen, it may be the first teeth coming through. This can happen at any time. Some babies are actually born with a tooth in place! The pain of teething can be relieved with a topical analgesic or a teething ring.

telephone

Q: How does your baby know when to cry loudly? A: When your telephone rings, of course. When you're on the phone, all of your attention is focused away from your baby. Well, your baby wants attention. He or she is thinking, "Hey, where did Dad go?"

Be vigilant even when you're on the phone. Your baby will try to get outside, paint a wall with fingernail polish, tip a hot frying pan over, eat the cat food, or worse, try to drink something poisonous from under the kitchen sink. When on the phone and watching your baby, announce right up front, "I may fade in and out on you here— I'm watching the baby."

television

Don't let the television become your babysitter, plopping your baby down in front of the screen for hours at a time. Is there anything wrong with your baby becoming enamored with a favorite television character? Maybe not, but statistics tell us that children now watch an average of five to seven hours of television a day. So many other wonderful activities can engage you and your child together. Read to and with your toddler. Begin with simple story or picture books. Try puzzles, building toys, simple games, and sing-along songs. Take your toddler to the local library for story time. Don't allow your little one to become a televisionaholic. Nothing can take the place of live human interaction.

thrush

Thrush is a fungal infection characterized by whitish patches on a baby's tongue or cheeks. Mild cases of thrush resolve without treatment, while more extensive cases require a doctor's care. If Mom is breastfeeding, the nipples need to be treated along with the baby; otherwise Mom and Baby can keep passing the thrush back and forth to each other.

thumb sucking

Here's another hot topic. Should you allow your baby to suck his or her thumb? Some say, "No problem, the kid'll grow out of it." Others announce, "How dare you ruin that baby's teeth!" Remember, babies have a very strong natural sucking instinct.

Some pediatricians recommend a pacifier since it can be removed when teeth begin to appear, whereas a thumb is just too handy for sucking. If your baby has a severe problem with thumb sucking, you can purchase an over-the-counter liquid that can be put directly on the thumb. It tastes terrible and will quickly stop the thumb sucking.

trimester

This is the term for a period of three months. Since pregnancy lasts nine months, it is the term used for the three parts or stages of pregnancy. Your doctor will take different approaches to your wife's care depending upon which trimester she is in.

tubal ligation (*see also* birth control)

This is a surgical sterilization procedure in which a woman's fallopian tubes are cut and tied off to prevent pregnancy. If you are considering tubal ligation, discuss this option with your doctor to identify any risk factors. Since tubal ligation is considered a permanent form of birth control, couples will want to prayerfully discuss it since it effectively ends childbearing.

twins

See multiples.

U

ultrasound

This procedure uses sound waves to create a moving image of internal organs. During pregnancy, ultrasound is routinely used to monitor the health and development of your baby. It also plays a major role in the assessment of the size of your baby and the duration of the pregnancy. It will not harm your wife or your baby.

You may not be able to attend every one of your wife's doctor appointments, but make as many as you can—this is a team project you've started! You'll certainly not want to miss an ultrasound. Technology has developed to such a degree that you can now see your baby fairly clearly on some ultrasound machines. Plus, you can hear the heartbeat and usually are allowed to videotape the entire session for future watching. Seeing and listening to your baby before he or she is even born gives fresh meaning to Psalm 139:13–16, where King David writes,

You formed my inward parts;

You wove me in my mother's womb.

I will give thanks to You, for I am fearfully and wonderfully made;

Wonderful are Your works,

And my soul knows it very well.

My frame was not hidden from You,

When I was made in secret,

And skillfully wrought in the depths of the earth;
Your eyes have seen my unformed substance;
And in Your book were all written,
The days that were ordained for me,
When as yet there was not one of them.
(NASB)

ultraviolet rays

See sunburn.

umbilical cord

The umbilical cord is the tissue that connects your baby from his or her navel to the placenta, carrying oxygen and nutrients to the fetus and transporting waste products away. At birth, an umbilical cord, which contains two arteries and one large vein, can be as long as four feet. After delivery, your doctor may ask you, Dad, if you want to cut the cord. We mention this to you now because it can be a surprise if you're not prepared for the question. After the delivery of our second-born, the doctor handed Paul a large pair of medical scissors and said, "You wanna cut him loose?" It was like cutting through a rubber garden hose. Dad, are you planning to cut your baby loose from Mom? You'll want to discuss this with your doctor and with Mom prior to the delivery.

uterus

Also called the womb, this is the hollow, pear-shaped organ in which your baby grows. During pregnancy, the fist-sized uterus goes from weighing about 2 ounces to weighing about 2.5 pounds and stretches to hold your baby.

V

vacations (*see also* air travel)

It's time for your annual summertime vacation! Are you all packed and ready to go? Wait a minute—the minivan is full, and you don't even have any of Baby's items on board yet. Traveling with a baby for the first time can be a real trip. Dad, you will play the role of loader and unloader. Keep in mind that the more stops you have on the agenda, the more loading and unloading you will be doing. Deciding what to take and what to leave behind can become as important as deciding on your final answer at the $64,000 level on *Who Wants to Be a Millionaire?* Should you bring the stroller? What about the portable crib? How many diapers? How much formula? Baby blankets, clothes, toys, diaper bags, playpen, and bottles—should you pack all of these items as well?

Most new parents pack too much stuff. The more trips you take, the more savvy you become in learning what to bring and what to ditch. This packing adventure becomes especially tricky with air travel. Since the rules are changing, we advise calling ahead to ask which items can be carried on and which need to be checked. Vacation with Baby can work, but careful planning is essential.

vacuum extraction

If labor does not progress, a vacuum extraction may be utilized.

A soft, rubbery oval ring will be placed on the baby's protruding head. The heavy suction of the vacuum will help pull the baby out. This may cause your baby to experience a cone-shaped head following delivery, but again, anything that will bring Baby out alive and kicking should not be dismissed. After a few days, your baby's head should round out nicely.

varicose veins

Varicose veins are swollen veins, usually in the legs, and are a common by-product of pregnancy because of increased blood volume, pregnancy-induced relaxation of the muscle tissue of the veins, and increased pressure on the veins from the growing uterus. Women who tend to be overweight and those who smoke are more likely to have varicose veins.

vasectomy

In the days after delivery, you may begin to consider some form of birth control. One of the two tubes in males that carry sperm from the testicles to the penis is called the *vas deferens*. When a man has a vasectomy, this tube is severed, preventing sperm from being ejaculated. While the procedure can sometimes be reversed surgically, it's generally considered a permanent form of birth control.

vernix

You have no doubt seen photos of a newborn taken in the moments immediately after delivery. Have you noticed the cheesy or waxy substance that coats the baby? In the uterus, vernix protects the baby's skin from exposure to amniotic fluid. Premature babies will be covered with vernix, while post-term babies will show almost none.

video

Many couples wish to preserve their delivery experience on video to show family, friends, and their own child someday. We recommend the G-rated version as opposed to the "nature's own wild kingdom" variety, so keep it modest. The goal is to tell the story of your baby's birth. You may want to take some video snippets in the days leading up to the birth. Then, you can add the story of the birth by filming a few minutes every hour or so while you are at the hospital. Finish off your production by including the coming-home segment, and you'll have an Academy Award–winning video that would make Steven Spielberg proud.

vitamins

Check with your doctor about your wife's taking vitamins once you find out you're expecting. There are some supplements like folic acid that are recommended to help prevent some birth defects.

vomiting (*see also* dehydration, spit-up)

In the beginning stages of breastfeeding or bottle-feeding, learn the difference between common spitting up, reflux, and real vomiting. If your baby spits up consistently after feedings, he or she may have reflux.

Because vomiting causes heavy loss of bodily fluids, it is especially dangerous in infants and toddlers. Do not take vomiting lightly. Call your pediatrician with the details. He or she may prescribe a nutritional supplemental drink or ask you to bring your baby into the office for an evaluation.

....

A Special Late-Night Delivery
Bill Donahue

I love being a dad. And there's nothing more exciting than experiencing the birth of a baby. Let's roll the tape back a few years to the birth of our daughter and let her tell the story from her perspective, perhaps a few days after she was born . . .

Hi! I'm Kinsley Anne, and on the eve of my birth, Mom got the normal pains and Dad called the hospital. By the time everyone was in the car, I was causing Mom great distress. But it wasn't my fault. You try living nine months in a dark, wet broom closet, and you'd be kickin' and screamin' too! (Remember, the way out of there isn't exactly a four-lane highway. Actually, it's kind of like forcing a grapefruit through a garden hose.)

We arrived at the emergency room at 1:25 AM. I heard the nurse tell Mommy, "Let's go! I'll get the paperwork." By this time, I really wanted out. My head was beginning to take on the shape of a gourd, and Mom was making lots of noise. It got real intense there for a while. I noticed that some food Mom had swallowed for dinner was going back out the way it came in. Whoa! This got everyone's attention. The nurse took Mom upstairs to the birthing room while Dad went to park the car. But, instead of just parking, Dad took a few minutes to comb his hair, talk to the staff, grab a soda—the usual male stall tactics.

They checked Mom into the birthing room at 1:42. I heard her ask for an epidural for the pain, but the nurse said, "Sorry, ma'am, you're too far along!" (Let's not talk about my mother's reaction to that!) Her doctor was not there yet, so the ER doctor showed up. He tried to look calm, but the puddle forming next to his shoes blew his cover. He was the new kid on the block and scared to death.

Mom yelled, "Where's my doctor!" In desperation, she grabbed the attending nurse's hand, ordering her to "stay here," which meant, "If you even think about leaving, I will keep your arm as a souvenir!" Dad arrived about 1:50 AM with a sleeping bag, tape recorder, food, and blankets. He looked like a Cub Scout in search of a den mother.

Meanwhile, the ER guy had his fingers up my nose, and I was thinking, "Yo! This isn't a mine shaft, it's a breathing device!" Next, he started squeezing my head like you check a football for air. I swore that I would bite his finger off if I got hold of it. But, without teeth, the best I could hope for was to gum him to death.

Finally, a woman obstetrician who had just delivered a baby next door came and offered to help get me out. ER Joe stepped aside, his ego shattered. (Better his ego than my body. After all, I knew a woman would get it right!) She eased me out promptly at 2:00 AM. Dad cut the cord, and then in walked Mom's doctor. Thanks, pal! (We named the placenta after him.)

Wow! What a night!

Well, as you can see, it was an adventure for Kinsley—and us! Her dramatic, eighteen-minute arrival and her early years have taught me many lessons. Here are a few:

- First, create moments with your kids. Do what you can to bring adventure, humor, love, and excitement to their lives. Initiate. Enter their world, even if it's not your size.
- Second, seize moments. Remember, this is the day. This is the moment—and you only have it once. It may be unplanned and it may be crazy, but it's all you have. God is showing up now, and you don't want to miss it.
- Third, mark significant moments. Turn moments into memories. We keep a victory candle and journal in the kitchen. We write down great moments, light the candle, pray, sing a few choruses to mark the

moments with our kids. Choose your own method, but be sure to seize the day—and your regrets will be few.

Dr. Bill Donahue is an author and leadership consultant who lives in Dundee, Illinois.

walking

Just as a baby rarely arrives on the due date, so too your toddler will decide to walk when he or she is good and ready. Don't fret over the timing. A baby who walks early is no guarantee of a future Olympic track star, just as a baby who walks late is not destined to always be late. We have five kids, and they all began to walk at different ages, some very early and one very late. Don't let others convince you that your baby should be walking by a magic date.

Baby's early attempts at walking are painful to watch. The process usually begins with crawling. Slowly, your baby will learn to pull himself or herself up on furniture and large play toys. This will ensure many black eyes and bumps on the head. It's unavoidable. If someone at the mall gives you a stony stare, feel free to enlighten that person with a comment such as, "Uh . . . he's learning how to walk like his dad."

water breaking

You may have heard funny stories about a pregnant woman's water breaking. But actually, the release of amniotic fluid is no laughing matter. It doesn't happen to all moms prior to delivery, but when it does it might start as a trickle of warm fluid and build to a large amount of fluid. If this happens, call the front desk of the maternity ward . . . and fast. Do not go shopping at the mall, do not get the car serviced, don't even finish watching the baseball game, because you're about to become a dad. When the water breaks, things really start to move. It's dangerous to delay getting to the hospital once the amniotic fluid starts to flow. But since you've read this book, you'll of course calmly gather the items you've already packed, drive along the predetermined route, and check into the maternity ward—only to find that your wife has spilled a large Diet Coke in her lap. (Just kidding about that last part.)

In the final month, your ob-gyn can give you some pH balance strips that you can dip into the fluid to make sure it's really amniotic fluid and not urine.

wean

When to quit breastfeeding is a highly personal decision. Some moms stop after a month or two. Others feel fine with feeding for a year or more. Dad, help your wife decide on a good stopping point—then support her in the decision. Some moms, for various reasons, feel pressure to either wean or to continue for some specific amount of time. Take the pressure off by assuring her she's doing a wonderful job of nursing. As long as your baby is gaining weight and your wife is happy with breastfeeding, there's no reason she shouldn't continue. Don't let others overly influence her by their protestations of "Well, no wonder he's small, you only breast-fed him for one month!" or "My goodness, if you don't stop nursing that girl, she'll never leave your side." These frivolous comments should be ignored.

welcome (*see also* announcements, yard sign)

Have you planned what type of welcome home your baby will receive? Think through some of the following questions and issues before dismissing the importance of this topic. Will family members or friends be present? Which ones? Will a family member or friend stay at your home for a time to help provide care? How long do you anticipate that person will stay? Can neighbors drop in for the big arrival? Will you have a sign in the yard or any other type of announcement for the neighbors? Plan now for the arrival of your newest family member. Think about it: your house will not be the same. There won't be "just the two of us" for many years to come. You'll only welcome your new baby home once, so do it right. Be careful using social media. We recently learned of a couple who posted, "Baby is coming . . . headed to the hospital," only to return home two days later and discover that someone had broken into their home.

well-baby checkups

In addition to the times when your baby is sick and needs to see your pediatrician, you also will schedule regular appointments to monitor your baby's health and development. Information covered usually includes the baby's height, weight, immunizations, developmental guidelines, screening tests, safety, and nutrition.

wet wipes

Buy stock in your favorite company that manufactures these wonders. Wet wipes work on everything. Buy them by the case. With a baby in tow, you'll constantly be reaching for a wet wipe. Babies and spills go together like peas and carrots (which happen to be two of the items constantly being spilled). There will be times when you can't access water, yet wet wipes are moist enough to wipe off your baby from runny nose to dirty toes. Wet wipes are your friend.

X-ray

Since exposure to X-rays may be harmful to a developing fetus, your pregnant wife should discuss her condition with doctors and her dentist before having any X-rays.

yard sign (*see also* announcements, welcome)

Nothing announces your joy like a giant yard sign. You can rent one or make your own. This sign serves several purposes. It lets all the neighbors in on your news at the same time. It's great fun to pose for a picture beside the sign with your newborn and wife when you return from the hospital. (In the future, when your child sees these pictures, he or she will realize how excited both of you were in your anticipation of his or her birth.) Dad, a little planning is in order. Don't spend coming-home day driving around town searching for the best deal on renting or buying a sign. Do your homework ahead of time and be ready for the big day! In our opinion, colorful, personalized signs with balloons, banners, or streamers look best.

Z

zealot

Be on the lookout for this person. There are zealots in many areas of child birthing and child rearing. Folks will tell you, "You simply MUST deliver your baby in your hot tub!" Or, "We can't believe you've decided to stop breastfeeding already!" You may encounter zealots who tell you how to educate your one-year-old and zealots who warn you about the dangers of taking your baby to worship for fear of catching pneumonia. And yet . . . God has given you the wisdom and insight to make decisions for yourself. Don't let parenting piranhas spoil the joy and excitement of raising your infant. The best way to fend off these expectancy experts is to humbly answer, "Well, thanks for that viewpoint; we'll certainly take that into consideration as we make our decision."

zinc oxide

See sunburn.

zoo

Babies love going to the zoo. It's a great way to get out for the day. You'll love watching how big your baby's eyes get when he sees the strange shape of a giraffe or an elephant. Don't let your baby reach his hands through the cages, however. Your infant may think the lion is *soooo* cute, but to the lion your baby's fingers look like an afternoon snack. We were at an animal park once when an elephant stuck his trunk through the bars and pulled a stroller up into the air . . . with our friend's baby strapped inside! This story sounds funny, but we can assure you that it wasn't at the time.

....

The Story of a Father and a Son
Paul Pettit

The story of Christianity is really a story about a Father and His Son. Once you become a dad, you'll understand the impact of the Good News—the story of Christianity—more clearly than ever before.

Christianity teaches that God is not one person, but three. Never created, existing eternally, the Godhead is made up of the Father, the Son, and the Spirit. You see, God created man to fellowship with Him and to reflect His glory. Yet, as you may have read, man fell short of this task. Thus, both the unbroken fellowship and the reflected glory were cut off. Left in this terrible state, man would have never reconnected with his Maker.

But—and this is where the Good News come in—the Father sent His Son to restore this broken relationship. You and I have access to the Father because of what the Son accomplished while He was here on earth. The Son, like the Father, was perfect in all ways. And yet the Son's perfection wasn't recognized by everyone while He was here on earth. The religious leaders of that day felt threatened by the Son's teaching and had Him killed. The totally innocent, loving Son was crucified on a Roman cross so that you and I could overcome our horrible state of being alienated from God.

As you gaze at your son or daughter, can you imagine willingly handing him or her over to be killed? Think what that act must have meant for the Father and the Son. Yet the Son, Jesus Christ, laid down His life willingly so that we could receive the ability to live forever. Dad, have you yet come to a point in your life where you have connected with your Father in heaven? There is no other way to make the connection than to believe in the Son.

In the introduction to this book, we told you about the father wound, or the pain one feels from being emotionally or physically disconnected from one's dad here on earth. Well, there is a father wound even greater than that: being disconnected from your heavenly Father. While your own father here on earth may have disappointed you by falling short in certain areas, your heavenly Father has done all He can to provide for your every need. Think of it: He sent His very own Son, His only Son whom He loved very much. He loves you, too, and has the very best in store for you if you will trust Him. The following is a sample prayer you could pray to overcome your distance from God:

Dear Father:

Thank You for sending Your only Son to die for me. I receive Jesus Christ now into my life to forgive me of all my sin. I thank You that You love me just as I am. Help me to trust You more and more as I become a follower of Your Son. I understand that I am no longer spiritually dead but alive forever through the death, burial, and resurrection of Jesus Christ. Amen.

An illustration of this good news can be seen in a story from our historical past.

A young man was visiting our nation's capital, Washington, DC, for the very first time. Since this young man possessed leadership gifts, he felt a strong urge to visit the capital's center of power, the White House, where the president of the United States resides.

As visitors walked past the stately mansion, some paused to sit in the green grass, taking in the scene in all its wonder and awe. Others stopped for a moment's glance, then hurried on to gaze at the next historic site. The young visitor was overwhelmed by the greatness and glory of the White House and couldn't stop staring. He even decided to forego the remainder of his tour and sit down on the front lawn to enjoy his boxed lunch. He was mesmerized, watching as much as he could of the activities in and around the White House. The young man longed to get closer, but he knew the barriers and guards standing sentry were not to be crossed.

In the afternoon, a small boy approached and asked why the young man was staring so intently.

He replied, "This is my first trip to the capital. I've heard about the White House all my life, but I still can't believe I'm really sitting here looking at it!"

At that, the little boy stretched out his hand toward the visitor and said, "Follow me, I'll take you inside."

Not wanting to disappoint such a little boy, the young man decided to go along with the game as far as it would take them. To the young man's shock, the little boy strode right up to the guards and, without even pausing, walked right past them. The young man held on tight as his heart began to race. His mind whirred, "Will we be arrested and thrown into jail?"

As the two approached the pristine, manicured gardens, the young man allowed a glance over his shoulder. Down past the lawn, he saw the other visitors, whom he had just left, looking back up at him. Quickly he turned back toward the White House, lest someone point out what the two were doing. The young man's heart was now literally pounding as he was led to the very front door of the White House. The little boy looked up at his slightly older companion, smiled, and swung the front door wide open.

The young man caught his breath as he saw the beautiful wood floors and walls before his very eyes. Hanging everywhere were stunning oil paintings and shining crystal chandeliers. And, of course, there were more policemen and guards. Yet now, the police appeared friendly, and when they saw the little boy, they actually smiled.

The little boy led the astonished visitor through one hallway after another until they approached the inner sanctum of the House, the Oval Office. The little boy let go of the young man's hand and whispered to a secretary who was sitting at a desk in the hall leading to the Oval Office. The secretary nodded . . . and the boy raced back to grab the hand of the young man. In a moment the two were walking right into the most powerful office in the world. As the door creaked open, the young man's knees almost buckled. His hands were wet with perspiration. Behind the dark oak desk stood a tall, thin, bearded man who was studiously fingering a faded piece of parchment. The young man was face-to-face with the president of the United States of America.

You see, the little boy was Thomas "Tad" Lincoln. Because of the relationship he enjoyed with his father, the sixteenth president, Abraham Lincoln, he possessed the authority to walk right past the guards and straight into the very heart of the White House's Oval Office. And since the young man was with Tad Lincoln, he shared in that same authority.

Before Jesus Christ left this earth, He stated plainly, "All authority has been given to Me in heaven and on earth" (Matt. 28:18 NASB).

When you place your trust in Jesus Christ, just as the young man trusted the little boy, one day Jesus Christ will take you with Him to a place much greater than the White House. Jesus Christ has the authority to take you into heaven itself.

One time Jesus the Son was sitting with His followers discussing His future plans. He said,

> Do not let your heart be troubled; believe in God, believe also in Me. In My Father's house are many dwelling places; if it were not so, I would have told you; for I go to prepare a place for you. If I go and prepare a place for you, I will come again and receive you to Myself, that where I am, there you may be also. . . ." Thomas said to Him, "Lord, we do not know where You are going, how do we know the way?" Jesus said to him, "I am the way, and the truth, and the life; no one comes to the Father but through Me." (John 14:1–6 NASB)

That's the good news of the Father and the Son.

Index

For more information on Dynamic Dads, write:
Dynamic Dads
PO Box 1282
Rockwall, TX 75087
Or visit:
www.dynamicdads.com